WAKE UP, DARLING

BY ALEX GOTTLIEB

★

A COMEDY IN TWO ACTS

★

DRAMATISTS
PLAY SERVICE
INC.

To

POLLY AND STEVE

WAKE UP, DARLING was first presented by Gordon W. Pollock in association with Lee Segall and Richard Cook at the Barrymore Theatre, New York City, May 2, 1956. It was directed by Ezra Stone and the set was designed by Ballou. The cast was as follows:

MARTHA ....Kay Medford
JULIET ....Paula Trueman
POLLY EMERSON ....Barbara Britton
DEERFIELD PRESCOTT ....Russell Nype
DON EMERSON ....Barry Nelson
GLORIA ....Grace Raynor
1ST POLICEMAN ....Robert Downing
2ND POLICEMAN ....Richard B. Shull
GRANVILLE PRESCOTT ....Raymond Bramley
PENELOPE ....Ann Whiteside
MRS. JOHNSON ....Jean Arley

The action of the play takes place in the apartment of the Don Emersons on East 75th Street in New York City. The time is the present.

ACT I

SCENE 1: Late afternoon.
SCENE 2: Very late that night.

ACT II

SCENE 1: A morning several weeks later.
SCENE 2: Fifteen minutes later.
SCENE 3: That evening.

WAKE UP, DARLING

*This is the home of Don and Polly Emerson. It is the
lower floor of a brownstone house in the East Seventies,
with most of the rear facing on a small garden boxed in
by a high fence. A trellis or two are against the rear of
the fence. A tree is in the garden. The front door is R. C.
at the rear on a raised portion of the apartment. A safety
chain is on the front door. Steps lead down from this
platform in three places: R. to the bedroom, L. to the
kitchen, and R. C. to the living room area. The two doors
on the opposite sides of the room lead into a bedroom
U. R. and to the kitchen U. L. The bedroom door is
louvered in two sections. Tall windows form the wall between the apartment and the garden at L.; part of these
are made of sliding doors of glass leading into the garden.
An open iron railing separates the raised platform from
rest of room—railing runs L. to R. Since Don is an advertising man and a writer, the apartment is cluttered with
magazines, scripts and books. The section of the raised
platform at L. is used as a dining room. On this are a
table and three chairs. This table now has on it a portable
typewriter, paper, pencils, etc. Another larger chair stands
in the corner U. L., just above the steps leading down to
the kitchen door. The room is furnished in relaxed modern, with good lamps, easy chairs, and an ample couch. A
fireplace is D. R., with a bench and a cushion in front of
it. U. R., between the front door and the bedroom door
is a phonograph cabinet, with records on top and book-
shelves over it. The bedroom phone is on the phonograph.
A chair stands D. R., and two large hassocks stand R. C.
and C. a small table R. of the chair and R. of the steps
leading down to the living room area is a large brick*

planter full of green plants. On the platform just L. of the door are an umbrella stand with an umbrella in it and a small bench on which the actors deposit purses, hats, etc., a mirror is on wall above stand. L. of the bench, against the rear wall is a large cabinet used as a bar, and as storage space. The couch, piled with cushions, stands L. C. in the living room area, in front of the raised platform. A coffee table with boxes of cigarettes, lighters, ashtrays, etc., is D. S. of the couch. Between the couch and the platform is a storage cabinet for Don's scripts, typewriter, etc. The phone, which has a long cord, is on the coffee table. L. of the couch, and just R. of the steps leading down to the kitchen door is a low brick ledge. Part of the L. wall U. S. of the kitchen door is covered with framed pictures of Polly and reviews of the shows she's been in.

It is late afternoon. Martha, who has been a secretary for more years than she cares to admit, is at dining table U. L., typing Don's new play. A cigarette dangles from the corner of her mouth. Juliet, who is the part-time cook-maid-laundress, lies on the couch reading a page of Don's manuscript.

MARTHA. *(Pulling finished pages from the typewriter.)* Well, another day.

JULIET. It's a shame you have to read Mr. Emerson's plays when you type them.

MARTHA. *(Rising, douses her cigarette.)* Yeah, but I've fallen into the habit. Among other habits. Anything in the house to eat?

JULIET. Just bourbon. We ran out of Scotch.

MARTHA. *(Separating carbons and script pages at the table.)* Thanks, anyway. I'll go find a nice dark saloon and see if somebody picks me up.

JULIET. Isn't that kind of dangerous?

MARTHA. A man who goes into a bar alone knows he's taking a chance. *(The phone, on the coffee table in front of Juliet, rings. She leans forward, picks up phone, and speaks into it while she continues to peruse the script page.)*

JULIET. The Emerson residence. None of 'em's here. *(Martha Crosses R. to the front door, and gathers up her gloves and purse from bench by front door.*) Usually she's home long before this. (*Listens for a moment.*) Yes, ma'am. I'll write the message down. Yes, ma'am, the minute I hang up. So I won't forget. (*She hangs up, lies back comfortably on the couch to continue her reading.*)

MARTHA. (*Crossing L. to above Juliet, on the platform.*) Who was that?

JULIET. Nothing important. Long distance from Chicago.

MARTHA. You must have an awfully strong union. (*Juliet does not reply.*) Tell Mr. Emerson if he wants me, I'll be around the corner at Mahoney's. He can call me on the pay phone. The bartender knows me. Knows me? He's got a bowl of pretzels named after me. (*The front door bursts open, and Polly Emerson enters. She's a living doll in looks and personality, and at the moment she's bubbling over with excitement. She puts her hat, gloves and purse on the bench by the front door.*)

POLLY. I got the part of my life! I've made it finally! Isn't it wonderful? I'm going to get my big chance! (*A step R., on landing, looking toward bedroom.*) Where's Don? Is he home yet? I want him to be the first to know. (*Calls toward bedroom.*) Don darling!

MARTHA. I must remember to get some of those pills for myself.

JULIET. (*To Polly, as she rises and carries phone to the brick ledge at L., curling up the long cord.*) Mr. Emerson isn't home yet.

POLLY. Oh. Aren't you excited, Juliet?

JULIET. (*Flatly.*) Sure, I'm excited. Did you remember to shop for dinner?

POLLY. (*Coming down C. steps to R. of couch.*) Of course not. Since when do Broadway stars shop for their dinner?

MARTHA. Since when are you a Broadway star?

POLLY. Since this afternoon.

MARTHA. (*Crossing R. on platform.*) You should wait for the reviews. It's nice to have confirmation. (*Juliet goes up the L. steps, puts away the portable typewriter, and clears the dining table of papers and carbons, but leaves typed manuscript pages, papers, etc., putting them into cabinet behind couch.*)

POLLY. Don't be so blasé, Martha. How often does an actress go to an audition to read for a bit and get the starring role?

MARTHA. It happens in every M-G-M musical.

POLLY. I still can't believe it's finally happened. After several years in the theatre. Why, I never had more than a dozen lines before.

MARTHA. Now you've got thirteen?

POLLY. More. I talk all the way through this show. I never leave the stage once.

MARTHA. Oh, the life of Cornelia Otis Skinner.

JULIET. (*Going down* L. *steps toward the kitchen door.*) You should have remembered to shop. Well, it looks like frozen food again tonight. People used to cook dinner—now they just thaw it out. (*Exits into kitchen.*)

POLLY. (*Sits on* R. *arm of couch.*) I'm disappointed in you, Martha. Here I'm going to be a star and you're not happy for me.

MARTHA. For you, yes. But not for Don. How do you think he'll feel if you're in a smash hit every night while he's at home writing a smash flop? (*She comes down* C. *steps and sits on* C. *ottoman.*)

POLLY. Don loves me.

MARTHA. Will he love you as much when your take-home pay is twice as big as his, and your name's up in lights?

POLLY. (*Rises, entranced, facing front.*) My name in lights! "Polly Emerson in 'Melinda'!" I'll have to take a picture to send home to Mamma. She'll be so happy.

MARTHA. Why don't you use your maiden name and make her delirious?

POLLY. I better check and see if there're any messages. (*Polly goes to phone at* L. *on brick ledge. Martha removes her comfortable shoes, and proceeds to change them for her street shoes, which are in her commodious handbag.*)

MARTHA. When do you go into rehearsal?

POLLY. As soon as they have all the money. They only need $275,000.

MARTHA. How much have they raised so far?

POLLY. All but $250,000.

MARTHA. Well! They're practically in Philadelphia. (*Puts comfortable shoes in purse, then speaks seriously.*) Polly, is it really so important for you to be a success in the theatre?

POLLY. (*Turns to Martha.*) I can't let Mamma down. Ever since I took my first ballet lesson—I was only five then—she said I was going to be a star.

MARTHA. What did you expect her to say—"My little darling, you stink!"?

POLLY. Do you know what Mamma gave up for my lessons?

MARTHA. Papa?

POLLY. (*A step in.*) I owe it to her to make good.

MARTHA. You owe it to Don to start having babies.

POLLY. (*Sitting on* R. *end of couch.*) I didn't come to New York to have babies.

MARTHA. (*Rises, crosses to* R. *end of couch.*) Few of us do. You won't believe it, but even I came here for a husband and a career. All the way from Yonkers. I was going to be the world's best tap dancer and marry the world's richest man.

POLLY. You never told me.

MARTHA. (*Putting on earrings which she has taken from her purse.*) I found out I had rhythm in my fingers instead of my toes.

POLLY. You must have met some men who wanted to marry you.

MARTHA. Sure. But the ones I wanted to marry just wanted to sleep with me.

POLLY. What happened?

MARTHA. They did. (*She sits on* R. *arm of couch, speaks reminiscently.*) Maybe it was the way I was brought up, Polly, but sex was wonderful in those days. It was exciting and forbidden. Now they've written so many books about it that the kids take it for granted. Like brushing their teeth twice a day.

POLLY. Don and I don't.

MARTHA. Don't brush your teeth twice a day?

POLLY. No, don't take anything for granted.

MARTHA. You've been so busy trying to make good in the theatre—and Don's been so busy trying to make good as a playwright ——

POLLY. (*Interrupting.*) We're the happiest couple I know. We never fight about anything except my mother.

MARTHA. Don't you? With your dramatic classes at night, and with Don writing every evening, the only time you two spend with each other is when you go to bed.

POLLY. What's wrong with that?

MARTHA. (*With a twinkle.*) Oh, I'm not knocking it. (*Rises, starts for front door.*) Well, I better get started before the alcoholic content in my body gets dangerously low.

POLLY. (*Following, to corner of bannister.*) Don't you want to hear about the show I'm in?

MARTHA. The saloons close at 4 a. m. and it's already 5:30. I might not get a good seat.

POLLY. (*Demonstrating a dance step or two.*) It's a musical. I sing and dance in it.

MARTHA. It's always nice for the leading lady in a musical to sing and dance. Who wrote it?

POLLY. The most wonderful boy. He wrote the whole thing by himself. The book, and the words and the music. He's a Yale man.

MARTHA. What else?

POLLY. Imagine being only twenty-three and writing a hit show.

MARTHA. Imagine being only twenty-three! (*Goes up* C. *steps to front door to get her hat from bench.*)

POLLY. You'll love this boy, Martha.

MARTHA. I'm sure I shall, and Don'll be crazy about him. (*Putting on hat at mirror on partition at* L. *of landing.*) When is he coming to dinner?

POLLY. (*Astonished.*) Tonight. How did you know?

MARTHA. I wish I could stay, but I promised to get myself loaded. (*Polly has followed Martha up onto the platform, now she turns away* L., *toward the kitchen.*)

POLLY. I should tell Juliet we'll be three for dinner. Juliet!

MARTHA. (*At mirror.*) Sure. As long as you forgot to shop, it doesn't matter how many there isn't enough for.

POLLY. Juliet! (*Juliet enters* L. *from kitchen, wearing her coat. She crosses through the room and up the* C. *steps to the front door.*)

JULIET. I heard every word. About our dinner guest. (*To Polly.*) You take the phone while I shop. If there are any messages, don't forget to write 'em down.

POLLY. Yes, ma'am.

MARTHA. (*As Juliet stands directly behind her, opening front door.*) Have you got Scotch on your list?

JULIET. And soda.

MARTHA. Good girl. (*Juliet opens front door wide. It slams into Martha, throwing her against the partition. Juliet goes out, closing the door.*)

POLLY. Isn't she a jewel?

MARTHA. The Kohinoor diamond. (*She steps back, regards herself in the mirror. To her reflection.*) Well, good luck, you beautiful creature. (*Thoughtfully, to Polly.*) It's not too late, Polly.

POLLY. Too late for what?

MARTHA. To phone Stover of Yale, call off dinner with him, and talk Don into becoming a father tonight. Why, if I know anything about raising money for a musical, you could have a baby and enroll him in Ethical Culture before rehearsals even begin.

POLLY. I wish you'd stop trying to get me into maternity clothes.

MARTHA. I work on a percentage with Lane Bryant. (*She exits through front door. The bedroom phone, which is parked on top of the phonograph cabinet, U. R., rings. Polly hurries R. to answer it.*)

POLLY. Hello! Oh, hello, darling. . . . The audition? . . . Wait till you hear! . . . Don, I'll tell you all about it as soon as you get home. . . . Are you leaving now? . . . Good. I'll see you in a few minutes. (*After listening.*) I love you, too. (*Polly hangs up the phone, pulls cord from socket, clutches phone to her, and whirls off into the bedroom, R. The front doorbell rings. Then there is a knock at the door. O. S. from bedroom.*) Come in if the door's open! It usually is. (*The door opens, and Deerfield Prescott thrusts his head around the door, apprehensively. He looks like "Esquire" imagines the typical Yale man looks, except that this one wears heavy horn-rimmed glasses.*)

DEERFIELD. (*Tentatively.*) Hello. . . .

POLLY. (O. S. *from bedroom.*) Hi!

DEERFIELD. It's me. Deerfield Prescott. The man you asked to dinner. Am I early?

POLLY. (O. S. *from bedroom.*) Not at all. Make yourself at home. Have a drink.

DEERFIELD. (*Crossing down C. steps.*) Thanks, but I don't drink.

POLLY. (O. S. *from bedroom.*) How do you like the apartment?

DEERFIELD. (*Looking around.*) It's nice, but it makes me nervous.

POLLY. (O. S. *from bedroom.*) Nervous?

DEERFIELD. This is the first time I've ever been alone in an actress' apartment. But there has to be a first time for everything, doesn't there? (*When there is no answer, he turns to bedroom.*) Doesn't there? (*Polly pokes her head out of the bedroom far enough to reveal a bare shoulder.*)

POLLY. Would you mind if I took a shower before dinner? I'd feel so much fresher.

11

DEERFIELD. It's up to you.

POLLY. Did I tell you how wonderful I think your songs are?

DEERFIELD. (*Driven into* L. *corner of bannister by her appearance.*) Thanks, but I wish I had less talent and more guts. I haven't got any guts, you know.

POLLY. No, I didn't know.

DEERFIELD. I didn't have any at Exeter. And I had even less at Yale. I'm completely gutless. My mother's psychiatrist says it's because an upstairs maid took advantage of me when I was eleven years old.

POLLY. You must have been quite precocious for your age.

DEERFIELD. They tell me I didn't even put up a struggle.

POLLY. No wonder your writing has so much depth. (*Deerfield crosses quickly up* C. *steps to landing, and just as quickly down* R. *steps to confront Polly at bedroom door.*)

DEERFIELD. I can see you understand me, Miss Emerson. That's why I came here tonight. Even though Penelope tried to talk me out of it.

POLLY. Who's Penelope?

DEERFIELD. She doesn't know anything about men and women. She went to Vassar.

POLLY. You can tell me about her after I shower.

DEERFIELD. Sure, Miss Emerson. (*Polly retreats into the bedroom, closing the door. Deerfield turns to the phonograph cabinet and inspects some records, lying on top. The front door opens, and Juliet barges in with six cokes in a carrier and a bottle of liquor done up in a paper bag. Juliet slams the door shut and goes* L. *on landing through opening for the bar at* U. C. *behind partition. Deerfield turns at the sound, but Juliet has vanished behind the partition. She sets the cokes and the liquor down firmly on the bar. Deerfield turns again. Now he faces the landing,* C. *Juliet steps from behind partition toward the front door. She spies Deerfield. They hold on one another, like a couple of bird dogs.*)

JULIET. (*Suspiciously.*) Who are you?

DEERFIELD. I was asked here. For dinner. By Miss Emerson.

JULIET. You the one with the book and the words and the music? (*Deerfield crosses to* R. C.)

DEERFIELD. I only wrote it to keep from working for my father. I wanted to prove a rich man's son could have a mind of his own.

12

JULIET. (*Crossing down* C. *steps to* L. *of Deerfield.*) How does your father feel about you?

DEERFIELD. He says it's too late for a blood test to establish his paternity. Tell me something ——

JULIET. If it's something I know.

DEERFIELD. Do you like me?

JULIET. Not especially. Why?

DEERFIELD. I always make a bad first impression. Later, most people learn to ignore me completely. Do you mind if I sit down? (*Goes to* D. R. *chair.*)

JULIET. Go right ahead. I want to see how you sit down. That usually gives away the kind of a person a person is. (*Deerfield starts to sit, then he sees Juliet staring at him. He stops, with his derriere halfway down, and looks at her askance. Juliet shakes her head. Deerfield sits.*)

DEERFIELD. Well?

JULIET. (*Without expression.*) I better get started in the kitchen. (*Starts* L. *for kitchen door.*)

DEERFIELD. (*Rising quickly.*) Don't leave me here alone! I mean, when Miss Emerson comes out.

JULIET. (*Pausing.*) *Miss* Emerson?

DEERFIELD. I don't know her well enough yet to call her Polly. Have you been with her very long?

JULIET. Since she was a baby. I'm a present from her mother who couldn't stand me any more. What makes you so nervous about being alone with Miss Emerson?

DEERFIELD. I've always been nervous around women. Since a certain event when I was eleven years old. But I hope to get over it tonight. My nervousness, that is. That's why I'm here. (*Crosses up* C. *steps onto platform, looking into garden.*)

JULIET. (*Dubiously.*) I thought you came to dinner. (*Front doorbell rings.*) Got a dime? (*Starts up* C. *steps. Deerfield hands her a dime. She goes to open the front door. Deerfield moves* L. *along platform and exits through the open sliding doors into the garden.*) That must be the grocery boy. (*Opens door without looking into hall.*) Take 'em into the kitchen and —— (*Notices two shopping bags sitting on threshold.*) Those boys are getting smaller and smaller. (*Pockets dime. Picks up shopping bags, closes door.*) Do you want a leisurely dinner, or do you want to be rushed through it?

DEERFIELD. (*Comes in from garden and stands above dining table.*) Oh, I'm not the eager beaver type. Make it leisurely. Gives people a chance to get acquainted with each other. You wouldn't have any candles to set the stage, would you?

JULIET. (*Goes down c. steps and L. to kitchen door, carrying the shopping bags full of groceries.*) We got candles for when the fuse blows out. You can have those.

DEERFIELD. Thanks. I always like to do things in a theatrical way.

JULIET. You're welcome. But don't be surprised if this is your farewell performance. (*She exits into kitchen. Deerfield looks after her, then he notices Don's playscript lying on the table. He picks up a page, smiles, pulls it closer to his face, the smile fading. He reads from the script, incredulously.*)

DEERFIELD. (*Reading.*) "Why are you standing in front of that closet if no one's in there?" (*He puts down the script, disapprovingly, and moves away, back into the garden. The front door opens, and Don Emerson enters. He is in his early thirties, personable, and has the harried expression of a man working in a profession he does not enjoy. Don calls toward the bedroom.*)

DON. Darling! Are you home? Polly? (*He goes L. through opening in partition, and tosses his brief case on the dining table. He takes out his pipe, but is distracted from lighting it when his eyes fall upon the pages of his script on the table. He picks up the same page Deerfield examined. He smiles, sits at table, R. chair. Reading.*) "Why are you standing in front of that closet if no one's in there?" (*Nods, chuckles approvingly at his own work, fishes for a light for his pipe. Deerfield, who has watched all this from the garden, moves through garden doors up behind Don and just as Don brings his cigarette lighter to his pipe, Deerfield shoves his own lighted lighter under Don's nose. Don recoils.*) Don't ever walk up to anybody like that!

DEERFIELD. (*Moving above, to R. of Don.*) I'm sorry if I startled you. May I ask who you are?

DON. (*Rising.*) Why not?

DEERFIELD. All right, who are you?

DON. Let's do it the other way around. Who are you?

DEERFIELD. I'm Deerfield Prescott.

DON. (*After a pause.*) Well, go ahead.

DEERFIELD. I'm a playwright. I write plays.

DON. Who doesn't?

DEERFIELD. Actually, I've only written one play.

DON. Oh.

DEERFIELD. And actually it isn't a play. It's a musical about the Civil War.

DON. Oh?

DEERFIELD. The producers expect my father to put up the money, but they don't know my father.

DON. As a matter of fact, neither do I.

DEERFIELD. You've never heard of Granville Prescott?

DON. Shocking as it may seem. I—don't mean to pry, but exactly why are you here?

DEERFIELD. I have a date with Miss Emerson. A dinner date.

DON. (*Leans on rail, facing front.*) How nice. How very nice.

DEERFIELD. (*Assuming a similar stance.*) I think so. She's quite a dish.

DON. Quite. (*Confidentially.*) Tell me, what are your plans for tonight? Anything special?

DEERFIELD. (*Man-to-man.*) We're having dinner in—(*With a gesture expressing everything.*) and then—well, you know . . .

DON. Indeed, I do.

DEERFIELD. I hope you're not planning to make it a threesome. I'm not very good at handling these things.

DON. I'm afraid you'll have to try. My plans happen to be exactly like yours. (*With the same expressive gesture.*) Dinner in—and then—well, you know . . .

DEERFIELD. There must be some mistake. Are you sure your date is for tonight?

DON. (*Moving above Deerfield to R. of platform.*) That's what Polly told me when I left this morning.

DEERFIELD. (*Taken aback.*) You mean you were here all —— (*Pivots backward, a step down the C. steps. Facing Don.*)

DON. (*Interrupting.*) Only a cad would tell. And I happen to be one. (*Displays latch key.*) I even have my own key. Can you say as much?

DEERFIELD. (*Reaching for Don's key.*) Not yet.

DON. (*Pockets key.*) Did Polly give you a big build-up, or was she her usual impulsive self?

DEERFIELD. I don't think we spoke fifty words before she said, "Why don't you come over for dinner tonight?"

DON. For her, that was a big build-up. (*Opens front door.*) Now, my good man, would you like me to hail you a cab, or can you handle that yourself?

DEERFIELD. Are you sure this is your night with Polly?

DON. I've been held over by popular demand.

DEERFIELD. That may be, but not for long. (*Goes down C. steps and leans against foot of bannister.*) Even if I walked out of her life tonight, I'd walk back in tomorrow.

DON. (*Closes door.*) What makes you so sure?

DEERFIELD. She's going to be Melinda in "Melinda." That's the musical I wrote. (*Sits C. bassock.*)

DON. (*Surprised, comes down C. steps to R. of Deerfield.*) Let me get this straight. Polly's going to star in your show?

DEERFIELD. She was marvelous at the audition today. Have you ever seen her sing and dance and play a love scene?

DON. Not all at the same time.

DEERFIELD. I feel she has something. Something that's never been brought to the surface—a kind of latent passion that can be violent and yet puritanical. Have you ever had that feeling about her?

DON. Sometimes. In the middle of the night. But then I just roll over and it goes away. (*Goes to phonograph cabinet, straightens records.*)

DEERFIELD. I'd like to tell you why Miss Emerson is so right for "Melinda," but I don't suppose you know much about plays.

DON. No, I'm in the advertising game.

DEERFIELD. I hear it's fascinating.

DON. That's for sure. (*Crosses up R. steps to bar.*) Well, as long as you're determined to stay, why don't we have a drink? This may be an evening to remember.

DEERFIELD. An evening to remember? That's a good song title. Would you mind if I used it? (*Writes in small notebook.*)

DON. Help yourself. What's mine is yours, apparently. (*Juliet enters from kitchen, carrying place mats, plates, silver and napkins. She goes up L. steps and moves to dining table.*)

JULIET. (*To Don.*) I didn't hear you come in.

DON. But you did hear me when I left this morning, didn't you? (*Deerfield swivels around. Don indicates him to Juliet.*) Have you met Mr. Prescott?

JULIET. (*Getting busy at the table.*) And he's met Miss Emerson.

16

DON. He's been telling me. (*Turns to bar.*)

JULIET. When you see Miss Emerson, tell her some woman called from Chicago. Said she'd be here tonight instead of tomorrow.

DON. I'll do that. (*To Deerfield.*) What do you drink?

DEERFIELD. Anything, as long as it isn't liquor.

DON. You make everything so easy.

DEERFIELD. I have an ulcer. (*Rises.*) The doctors can't find it, but I know it's there. (*Crosses to above couch, standing below railing.*)

JULIET. (*To Deerfield, standing just above railing.*) Doctors! What do they know? I had an uncle once who drove the whole Mayo clinic crazy. He was dead and buried before they found out he was lying about where his pains were. (*Turns to continue setting the table.*)

DEERFIELD. (*Facing front, leans against railing.*) All my relatives are dull. Do you suppose that's because they're so rich?

DON. (*At bar.*) It does give them a helluva head start.

DEERFIELD. You're quite astute for an advertising man.

DON. Thanks.

DEERFIELD. What kind of work do you do?

DON. I write copy. Perfume ads. Any comment? (*Comes down to railing.*)

DEERFIELD. No, sir. I suppose someone has to do it.

DON. I convince five million women a year that romance comes out of a bottle.

JULIET. (*At L. end of dining table, gesturing with a fork.*) You don't convince me. I say that if a woman can't win a man with good soap and water, who needs him? (*Goes back to setting table.*)

DON. (*To Deerfield, as he returns to the bar.*) How do you stand on perfume?

DEERFIELD. You wouldn't believe what happens to me. When I get close to a girl who's wearing perfume, why, I take one good sniff ——

DON. (*Covering his eyes in mock protest.*) Please—not before dinner. (*Returns to Deerfield, coke bottle in one hand.*) I just realized something. You're it. You're exactly what I need for the third act.

DEERFIELD. Third act?

DON. Of my new play.

DEERFIELD. Oh, is that what you were laughing over before?

DON. I find myself hysterically funny. (*Don starts to pour the coke, but suddenly realizes Deerfield has no glass. He goes back to the bar for a glass.*)

DEERFIELD. Now I understand your relationship with Miss Emerson.

DON. I'm not so sure that I do.

DEERFIELD. I'll be happy to explain it to you.

DON. Oh, would you?

DEERFIELD. There's something about a playwright that attracts eager young actresses. We offer them the promise of a brighter tomorrow.

DON. (*Coming to railing with glass for Deerfield, and coke.*) That's good to know. Real good.

DEERFIELD. You probably met her just like I did.

DON. At an audition? (*Bitterly.*) Mr. Prescott, I am now on play Number 6 and not one producer has found the slightest merit in anything I've written. (*Pours coke.*) Say when.

DEERFIELD. That'll be fine.

DON. (*Puts half empty coke bottle on dining table. Goes back to bar, mixes his own drink and returns to above Deerfield with it.*) The ads I write are full of sex appeal, but I'm told my plays don't have any.

DEERFIELD. What's the name of your new one?

DON. "Without Passion."

DEERFIELD. (*Sipping coke.*) Why don't you put in a little?

DON. I spend six hours a day fifty weeks a year selling love and romance. Don't you think that's enough for one man? (*Drinks, at the same time pouring the rest of the coke into Deerfield's glass.*)

DEERFIELD. It would be for me.

DON. (*Goes to bar with his glass and empty coke bottle.*) I need another drink.

DEERFIELD. Do you think you should?

DON. Oh, there's nothing in these but whiskey. (*Fixes fresh high-ball.*)

DEERFIELD. (*Sits on the back of the couch.*) It must be quite discouraging to write plays that never get produced. I felt terrible after I finished "Melinda." It was four weeks before any producer grabbed it.

DON. (*Comes down C. steps to R. C.—his drink in his right hand*

—*a bottle of Scotch in his left hand.*) Must have seemed like a whole month. (*Raising his drink.*) Well, good luck with Polly.

DEERFIELD. (*Raising his drink.*) Well, good luck with your play. Looks like I've got what you want and you've got what I want. (*Rises and goes to Don.*)

DON. Looks like. (*They both drink. Juliet starts down L. steps on her way to kitchen.*)

JULIET. Table's set. Can you keep your voices up kind of loud while I'm in the kitchen? (*She exits into kitchen. Deerfield moves U. R. toward the bedroom door. He looks at his watch, gloomily.*)

DON. You look depressed. I hope it isn't because I'm hanging around.

DEERFIELD. I was counting on tonight.

DON. Me too.

DEERFIELD. (*Hopefully.*) Maybe you'll get sleepy after dinner.

DON. If I do, you'll be the first to know. (*The bedroom door opens, and Polly sweeps into the room in a ravishing hostess gown. Deerfield extends his arms to embrace her, but Polly runs up the R. steps, down the C. steps, and goes to Don at C. Deerfield turns front.*)

POLLY. Darling! Wait till you hear what happened to me at the audition! (*Don gives Polly a first-week-of-marriage kiss, keeping an eye on Deerfield, who grabs the Scotch bottle out of Don's hand and pours it into the glass of coke he carries.*)

DEERFIELD. To hell with my ulcer! (*Drinks.*)

POLLY. Donald! What's gotten into you?

DON. (*Bending Polly over his L. knee, which he places on C. ottoman.*) My love, my pet, my sweet! You were still asleep when I left this morning! (*Winks at Deerfield, knowingly, extends glass for Deerfield to pour him more Scotch, then buries his face in Polly's neck. Deerfield crosses above to L. of Don and Polly.*)

DEERFIELD. Miss Emerson . . . Miss Emerson, if there's been a mixup in dates, I'll be happy to come back tomorrow night.

POLLY. You stay right here! (*Pulls free of Don, and moves R.*) Don, stop biting me! What would my mother say?

DON. (*Following.*) The same thing she said when she caught us in the pantry six years ago.

DEERFIELD. (*Bewildered.*) This has been going on for six years?

DON. (*Takes bottle from Deerfield.*) This is nothing. You should see us when we're alone.

POLLY. Will you please let go of me long enough to introduce you to Mr. Prescott? (*She succeeds in pulling away.*)

DON. We've not only met, we've bared our souls to each other.

POLLY. Then he's told you the good news.

DON. That you're adopting him?

POLLY. No, this afternoon he discovered me.

DON. (*The all-purpose gesture.*) And he's planning to continue his explorations tonight!

DEERFIELD. (*Puts glass on coffee table.*) Now, wait a minute— you can't talk like that.

DON. (*Holds bottle, assumes a fighting stance.*) No?

DEERFIELD. (*Shakes finger at Don.*) If I had any guts ——

DON. (*Extends chin.*) It's an even match. I've got a glass jaw. (*Deerfield hesitates, then faces front, displaying closed fist.*)

DEERFIELD. Weak knuckles. They run in our family.

DON. Well, then, let me punch you!

POLLY. (*Coming between them.*) Please forgive him, Mr. Prescott. At his age, if he takes more than one drink before dinner ——

DON. (*Interrupting, insulted.*) At my age! Since when can't I hold my liquor? (*Pours fresh drink. Gives bottle back to Deerfield.*) Now, my dear girl, will you please tell me why we're breaking bread with this refugee from the Ivy League?

POLLY. Mr. Prescott happens to be a brilliant young playwright. I was hoping he'd be kind enough to tell you what's wrong with your plays.

DON. He already has. And he's so brilliant he did it without reading a word.

DEERFIELD. I did read one page, if you'll forgive me.

DON. How did you like it?

DEERFIELD. I thought it dragged a little.

DON. (*Caustically.*) I know just where. (*Extends hand, Deerfield puts the bottle into it.*) Good night, Mr. Prescott. You've been a big help to me, and on opening night there'll be two tickets at the box office in your name.

POLLY. Don, this is my home and I invited Mr. Prescott here as my guest.

DEERFIELD. It seems I ought to go.

POLLY. You're not going anywhere before dinner. Don probably likes you very much.

DON. Don adores him. And Don needs a fresh drink. (*Above table R., pours drink—puts bottle on table.*)

POLLY. Don needs a kick in the head.

DEERFIELD. No, he's right. He doesn't have to like me just because you do.

DON. Do you know why she likes you?

DEERFIELD. I know it isn't animal magnetism because I don't have any.

DON. (*Moves to R. of Polly.*) I'll tell you why. Because Polly's an actress. Morning, noon and night, awake or asleep, an actress dreams of only one thing. Success! If you've written a hit, and I have the sickening feeling that you have, then Polly's private dream of success is going to come true. (*Goes above R. table, refills glass, drinks.*)

POLLY. And I'll be eternally grateful.

DEERFIELD. But I don't want you if it's just out of gratefulness.

POLLY. You don't want me for what?

DEERFIELD. I'd rather not tell you in front of him.

POLLY. Leave the room, Don.

DON. I will not. And I'll tell you if he won't. He's crazy about you.

POLLY. (*Delighted.*) Crazy about me! Oh, that's impossible.

DON. Is it? Why, he hasn't been able to get you out of his mind since this afternoon. You're driving him mad, mad, mad!

POLLY. (*To Deerfield.*) You're really crazy about me?

DON. (*Mock astonishment.*) Isn't everybody?

POLLY. Shut up and give me a drink. A double. (*Both men start for the bar. Don darts up the R. steps and reproves Deerfield from the landing.*)

DON. Ah—ah! Tonight's my night! (*Goes to bar.*)

DEERFIELD. (*To Polly.*) Yes, I am crazy about you. But he is, too, isn't he?

POLLY. I suppose so, but he doesn't tell me very often. (*She links arms with Deerfield, leads him D. C.*) Husbands often forget that their wives are women. Even when they've been married only five years. (*Deerfield is open-mouthed in horror at Polly's revelation. Helplessly, he draws a thumb over his left shoulder to indicate Don, who grins cherubically at the bar. Slowly, Deerfield sinks on the C. hassock. He drops his head dramatically into his L. hand.*)

DON. (*Coming down C. steps with fresh drink for Polly.*) He's

21

obviously not a Noel Coward fan. (*Don moves above Deerfield, to his* L., *and pries open the fingers of his* L. *hand. He sets the drink into the fingers, lifts Deerfield's chin, tilts the drink to Deerfield's lips, forcing the drink into Deerfield, who sits dazed.*)

POLLY. Don, didn't you tell him we were married?

DON. Just never got around to it. Why didn't *you* tell him?

POLLY. I took it for granted I looked married. He certainly must have noticed my ring. (*Looks at* L. *hand, then hides it behind her.*) Oh, dear! I forgot I never wear it to auditions.

DEERFIELD. (*Starting to rise.*) Miss Emerson, this is a most ——

DON. (*Pushing him back down with one finger.*) *Mrs.* Emerson, if you don't mind.

POLLY. Let the man talk.

DEERFIELD. There's an old Bulgarian proverb that says a woman needs three husbands. One to support her, one to love her, and one to beat her. (*Drinks.*)

DON. (*Sits,* R. *arm of couch.*) How did we get to Bulgaria?

DEERFIELD. I assume you've been supporting her, and you've probably been beating her. (*Drinks.*)

DON. Can I help it if she likes it?

POLLY. Don!

DEERFIELD. All I want is to love her. You see, Mr. Emerson, ever since I was eleven years old, I've been looking for a girl who would stir me the way your wife stirred me when I first saw her today.

DON. (*To Polly.*) Tell me about it, darling.

POLLY. (*A step* U. S.) Honestly, Don, I didn't do a thing. I just stood on the stage and sang and danced.

DON. And stirred him up!

POLLY. I didn't even know who he was then. I thought he was just a fellow with glasses and a crew-cut.

DON. You must have done something to twist his little mind! (*To Deerfield.*) Exactly what are your future plans for my wife, if I'm not being too inquisitive?

DEERFIELD. (*Goes to Don.*) I'm going to take her away from you.

DON. Oh, let's not be evasive. Give me a straight-forward answer.

DEERFIELD. I mean it.

POLLY. (*Puts drink on planter,* R.; *then faces Deerfield.*) You do? You really do? (*She enjoys the situation.*)

22

DEERFIELD. I know what I want when I want it. And I want you.

POLLY. Isn't that nice! Say it again, just like you did.

DEERFIELD. I know what I want when I ——

DON. (*Interrupting.*) Oh, come now, what could you possibly want with an old hag of twenty-seven?

POLLY. Twenty-five!

DON. In the casting offices, maybe, but not in this house. And next month you'll be twenty-eight.

POLLY. (*Turns away, furious.*) You're horrible!

DEERFIELD. (*Goes to Polly.*) Don't be upset. Twenty-five or twenty-eight, it doesn't matter to me. I've always preferred older women.

DON. (*Crossing to chair R.*) Then you two were obviously made for each other. (*Sits, pours drink, puts feet on R. hassock.*)

POLLY. You're even more horrible than Mamma warned me.

DON. Remind me to tell you what I think of your mother.

POLLY. You've told me.

DON. Not often enough!

DEERFIELD. I promise to idolize your mother. She sounds charming.

DON. (*Pouring a little more into his glass from bottle on R. table.*) All secret drinkers are charming.

POLLY. Don! Mamma's never touched a drop in her life!

DON. (*Airily.*) I know, dear. Of course, she's the only woman who was ever blackballed by Alcoholics Anonymous ——

DEERFIELD. Her mother's alcoholic tendencies have nothing to do with our problem.

DON. What problem?

DEERFIELD. My infatuation for your wife.

DON. Oh, *that* problem. I'll be happy to forget you ever mentioned it.

POLLY. I won't. (*To Deerfield.*) Let me hear that part again about wanting me when you want me.

DEERFIELD. (*Crossing back of Don, to his R.*) I'll be happy to in a minute. (*To Don.*) You're not taking me seriously, are you?

DON. If I were you, God forbid—and you were me, would you?

DEERFIELD. Of course.

DON. You will tell me why?

DEERFIELD. Certainly. Because an actress is an actress first and

23

a wife second. You admitted that yourself, even though you didn't put it as well.

DON. I hoped you wouldn't notice.

DEERFIELD. (*Sits on* R. *table, facing Don.*) If Polly becomes a star, who'll appeal to her the most? A perfume copy writer with six unproduced plays, or the man who made her famous and is crazy about her besides?

POLLY. (*Crossing above, to* R. *of Don.*) And keeps telling her so. (*Enchanted.*) He's like a breath of spring, isn't he?

DON. I'm a fall and winter man myself. You don't really believe what he said?

POLLY. He's giving me a chance to become a star. Don't you want me to become a star?

DON. (*Rises, crosses* C.) A star! You can be the Little Dipper and the Big Dipper and the whole damn Milky Way as far as I'm concerned! But how in heaven's name can a fellow his age with 10-10 vision walk in and steal a man's wife just because his combination of genes and chromosomes enables him to write words and music?

POLLY. And the book.

DEERFIELD. I can see it all as clearly as when I compose. This was meant to be. It's fate.

DON. Now why can't I write lines like that?

DEERFIELD. (*Toasting Polly with his drink.*) To you, Melinda.

POLLY. Melinda! Isn't that a beautiful name?

DON. (*Going* L. C.) It is not only a hideous name, but I forbid you ever to mention it again in this house. I may not even let you be in the show!

POLLY. And how are you going to stop me?

DON. (*Darkly.*) I'll find a way! (*Juliet enters from the kitchen, wearing a freshly starched cap, and carrying two unmatched kitchen candles stuck into the tops of wine bottles. The candles burn brightly, as Juliet goes up the* L. *steps toward the table.*) What the hell are those for?

JULIET. Dinner. In case a fuse blows out. (*Deerfield gives Polly his arm, escorts her up the* C. *steps, as Don looks on in amazement.*)

CURTAIN

ACT I

Scene 2

The room is dark except for light from the open bedroom door. Clean glasses and a bottle of liquor are back on the bar. A basket of fruit, including a banana, is on the coffee table. The drapes are closed across the windows on the garden.

Don, wearing pajamas, and wrapped in an electric blanket, is huddled on the couch. He turns over, miserably, and his bare feet pop out. He moves his pillow from the R. end of the couch to the L., and tries again to get comfortable.

POLLY. (*From bedroom.*) Don! (*After a moment.*) Don, are you awake?

DON. No, I'm asleep.

POLLY. (*From bedroom.*) You can't be. I hear you talking. Come to bed.

DON. I am in bed.

POLLY. (*From bedroom.*) You can't be comfortable. (*Don rises, gets both hassocks and puts them together between the coffee table and the couch to form an addition to his narrow bed.*)

DON. Oh, yes, I can. I've just realized what a miserable invention the double bed is. Especially if you're trapped in one with a wife with cold feet. This is the only way to get a good night's rest. (*Don tries to lie down on the improvised bed, and falls between the two hassocks onto the floor. Polly enters from bedroom, in pajamas, crosses to above the couch, as Don picks himself up and lies down on the couch with his head at the L. end.*)

POLLY. Want me to tuck you in?

DON. (*Pulling the blanket around him.*) I'll thank you to get out of my room. (*Polly turns on a lamp over Don's head.*) Turn off that light!

POLLY. I want to talk to you.

DON. (*Covering his eyes, as if he were the victim of the third*

25

degree.) All right, I'll talk! I'll talk! But I want you to know we have nothing in common after what you did tonight.

POLLY. (*Leaning over back of couch.*) What did I do?

DON. A man needs a wife who doesn't drool when another man —in front of her husband, no less—tells her she's the living reincarnation of Cleopatra, Marie Antoinette and Catherine the Great. Really!

POLLY. (*Doing a "star" walk* D. L.) He did get carried away, didn't he?

DON. Not far enough. And what he said about my plays! (*Polly sits on the* L. *end of the couch. Don draws away.*) Go away, Cleopatra, I need my sleep.

POLLY. Don, I want to talk to you about us.

DON. What for? The boy wonder already settled everything. You heard him at the dinner table. After you become a star, you'll leave me for him and I'll become a lonely but successful account executive.

POLLY. (*Moving closer.*) Do you want me to leave you for him?

DON. And the way he ate my food! Of course I don't want you to leave me! You'd think he hadn't eaten for weeks.

POLLY. His father cut off his allowance two months ago.

DON. What's he been living on all this time?

POLLY. The allowance from his mother.

DON. (*With heavy sarcasm.*) I will say this for you. You were most firm about not kissing him good night.

POLLY. He looked so woebegone when he left. Maybe I should have.

DON. That does it! (*Don rises, goes up* C. *steps, turns on light by the bar, and fixes himself a drink.*)

POLLY. Do you really believe I'd have an affair with him?

DON. No, but you probably will.

POLLY. Now what does that mean?

DON. It means I know a lot more about women than you do about men.

POLLY. Do you? Why, he couldn't get to first base with me.

DON. He will.

POLLY. Maybe you and I have different ideas of where first base is.

DON. We certainly have. Tonight—at that table and right before my eyes—who said she'd be delighted to run over his songs with him at his apartment?

POLLY. What's wrong with that? He happens to have a piano and we don't.

DON. His piano happens to be first base! It isn't far from running up and down the scales to running around the bases. (*Polly sits on the back of the sofa, peeling a banana, which she has picked up from basket on the coffee table.*)

POLLY. Don, do you really think I would?

DON. (*Coming down* C. *steps and crossing to* R. *of Polly behind the couch.*) Would what?

POLLY. Be unfaithful to you.

DON. (*Sits on back of couch from upstage side.*) Don't be so damned old-fashioned. Of course you would. Why should you be different? In the wrong circumstances with the right man, every married woman can be tempted.

POLLY. I never have been. Do you suppose there's something wrong with me? Like too many morals and not enough hormones?

DON. No, with you I think it's simply not enough opportunity. Did anyone ever tell you before that you were more desirable than Ava Gardner?

POLLY. Yes.

DON. I don't believe it. Who?

POLLY. You. Before we were engaged.

DON. I only said it because I wanted to marry you.

POLLY. Was I more desirable than Ava Gardner?

DON. How do I know? I was in love.

POLLY. Aren't you any more?

DON. A man stays at the boiling point only so long. That's what intrigues you about Deerfield. His thermometer runneth over.

POLLY. Oh, relax, Don. He's just a nice boy.

DON. (*Rises and crosses around* L. *of couch.*) With a man's ideas. And a great big unholy yen for you. Have you ever been alone in an apartment with someone who adores you madly? (*Sits* L. *end of couch.*)

POLLY. (*Slides down beside him.*) I'm in one now. And you adore me madly, don't you?

DON. I'm different. I'm your husband.

POLLY. (*Puts pillow in Don's lap and lies down on it.*) Deerfield's just as harmless.

DON. (*Gagging on his drink.*) What does that mean?

POLLY. Now don't get insulted. Like you said, a husband cools off. I don't expect you to be on the prowl night after night. (*Turns over.*)

DON. Well, you certainly picked a fine time to start complaining.

POLLY. I'm not complaining. All I'm saying is that you don't have any fangs and neither does he.

DON. And neither does a double-barreled shotgun until someone aims it at a moose and pulls the trigger. In this case, Miss Emerson, you're the moose!

POLLY. *Mrs.* Emerson.

DON. Mark my words, you'll be in and out of his piano before you know it.

POLLY. I say I won't. What do you want to bet on it?

DON. Bet? If I win, I lose.

POLLY. (*Sits up.*) Well, let's suppose for a minute that you're right. What do you want me to do—tell Deerfield I won't play Melinda because you're afraid I can't resist him?

DON. No, tell him the truth. Tell him you don't have enough talent for the part.

POLLY. (*Rising.*) I don't have enough talent! (*Pushes* R. *bassock to* R. C.) Donald Waldo Emerson, if I thought you meant that!

DON. And if I do?

POLLY. That does it! Now you can sleep on the couch for the rest of your life! (*Polly starts for bedroom, Don puts down drink on coffee table, rises, catches her by the arms.*)

DON. What did you want to talk to me about?

POLLY. (*Kneeling on remaining bassock between couch and coffee table.*) Let go of me so I can slug you. (*Struggles.*)

DON. What was so important that you got out of a nice warm bed?

POLLY. (*Evasively.*) It wasn't important.

DON. That means it was.

POLLY. It was silly. Silly and idiotic. This was the first time since we got married that you didn't kiss me good night.

DON. Kissing breeds germs.

POLLY. We've got a medicine chest full of wonder drugs.

DON. It's not worth the risk. Not unless you're in love.

POLLY. Why don't you kiss me and find out if we are?

DON. (*Pulling away, but Polly clings to him still.*) A married man doesn't kiss his wife in her pajamas in the middle of the living room.

POLLY. Deerfield wouldn't stand here and quibble.

DON. (*Holding her away.*) Are you going to be thinking of him when I kiss you?

POLLY. I never think of anyone when I'm kissing. I'm not that old yet.

DON. Okay then. Just this once. (*Just as they are ready to kiss, the phone rings.*) If that's your mother calling again —— (*Goes to phone on ledge.*)

POLLY. It's two hours earlier in Akron. But Mamma always thinks it's the other way around.

DON. In five years she's never called except when we're sound asleep. (*Polly pushes* L. *bassock* D. L., *goes to wall switch below kitchen door, turns on all the lights. Don, at phone.*) Hello . . . hello. . . . Who? (*Listens momentarily.*) No, Mr. Prescott isn't here. He left about an hour ago on Cloud 7. Who is this? (*Listens, his expression darkening.*) He was supposed to do what? (*Sits on ledge, Polly sits on* L. *steps, trying to overhear the conversation.*) No, young lady, he didn't—(*Changes phone to* R. *ear, Polly rising to follow behind him.*) and if he does, it will be over my dead body and his. Thank you no end. (*Hangs up and glares at Polly who looks at him in all innocence.*)

POLLY. Who was that?

DON. (*Standing, pointing at phone.*) That was a young lady named Penelope. She spent most of the afternoon trying to talk young Mr. Prescott out of spending most of the night with you. She said he said you'd do anything to get the part of Melinda. Is that what you said, my darling?

POLLY. (*Flustered, crosses below Don to* R.) You know what I said didn't mean what I said.

DON. (*Following.*) You could have fooled me.

POLLY. Making good in the theatre is important to me, but not that important.

DON. Okay. Prove it. Do something that's really important.

POLLY. Like what?

DON. Like having a baby.

POLLY. Don, you're tired and a little high.

DON. The perfect combination for seduction.

POLLY. Why don't we go to bed and talk it over? (*Polly tugs*

29

him toward bedroom, her hand wound up in the front of his pajama coat.)

DON. Well, that's a good way to start. (Pulls back, she releases him.) But so help me, if that moose hunter ever comes around here again, I'll give each of you one barrel.

POLLY. You haven't even got a double-barreled shotgun.

DON. I'll get one! (There is a loud knock at the front door. They both turn in surprise.)

POLLY. Who can that be?

DEERFIELD. (From hallway.) It's me, Deerfield. I have to talk to you.

DON. The moose hunter! Where's my army rifle?

POLLY. (Unthinking.) In the bedroom. (Don crosses above her for bedroom, she follows.) Oh, stop playing the outraged husband. You know that gun isn't loaded.

DON. Okay then—I'll bludgeon him to death! (Exits into bedroom, leaving his drink with Polly.)

POLLY. (Darting up R. steps to front door.) Go away. Please go away.

MARTHA. (From hallway.) Open up, Polly! I'm thirsty.

POLLY. (Bewildered.) Martha? I thought you were someone else. (She opens the front door. Martha enters with the dignity of the slightly stiff. The door remains open.) Are you alone?

MARTHA. (Looking over her shoulder, out into the hall.) I wasn't but I am now. (Sees drink in Polly's hand, goes for it.) Oh—I see you were expecting me! (Takes glass from Polly. Polly closes the door. Don bursts in from bedroom with his army rifle, ready for action. Martha turns to R. steps, finds herself looking into the barrel of the rifle. To Don.) I didn't know it was yours. Here. (Extends drink to Don. Don ignores her, brushes past the two women, going up R. steps and across platform, pushing aside drapes that are closed across windows U. L.)

DON. Where is he!

POLLY. He was only Martha.

DON. Don't try to throw me off the trail! After listening to that voice for five hours, I'd know it anywhere. What have you done with him?

MARTHA. (Moving down R. steps.) He sounds loaded.

POLLY. He's been like this all night. (Leans down toward Martha *from top of steps.*) I've become the most desirable female in the world ever since ——

DON. (*Crossing toward them, on platform.*) Not to me you're not! Only to Deerfield Prescott, boy home-breaker.

MARTHA. (*Crossing to above R. chair.*) He doesn't drink like a boy.

DON. He doesn't drink at all.

MARTHA. (*Puts hat and purse in R. chair.*) Oh, no? You ought to have a picture of the one we tied on tonight at Mahoney's.

POLLY. (*Crossing down C. steps toward Martha.*) Our Deerfield Prescott?

MARTHA. (*Leans against R. chair, kicks off shoes.*) There couldn't be two of him. He wandered into the bar about an hour ago and talked me into a drink. Six Scotches later . . .

DON. (*Interrupting.*) Where is he now?

MARTHA. Last I saw of him, he was lying out in the hall. (*Don opens the front door. Deerfield, quite potted, leans against the R. side of the door frame at a perilous angle.*)

DEERFIELD. (*Straightening up.*) Good evening. May I? (*Steps into the room.*)

DON. (*Closing door.*) May you what?

DEERFIELD. (*Navigating C. steps.*) Sit down. My legs seem to be made of jello. (*Goes to the couch.*)

POLLY. Martha, aren't you ashamed of yourself?

MARTHA. The older I get, the younger they get.

DEERFIELD. (*Lies down on couch, his head at the L. end.*) I do like a nice deep chair.

DON. (*Crossing to above couch, on landing.*) Now he's in my bed!

MARTHA. (*Crossing to bottom of C. step.*) What were you hunting in your pajamas?

POLLY. (*Pointing at Deerfield.*) Don was hunting him.

MARTHA. You'll have to do the sporting thing, Don. Wait and catch him on the rise! (*Don has crossed down L. steps to L. of couch. He picks up blanket from back of couch.*)

DON. (*To Polly, who moves toward him behind couch.*) Cover him up before his talent gets cold. (*Polly unplugs blanket from baseboard plug behind couch.*)

POLLY. Oh, stop making noises like a husband. And give me your Daisy Air Rifle.

DON. (*Proudly shouldering the rifle.*) It happens to be a Garand and we won the war with it.

POLLY. (*Takes gun from him, shoulders it.*) Of course we did. (*Turns to Martha.*) You're on sentry duty till I get back.

MARTHA. (*Salutes.*) Hup 2-3-4—hup 2-3-4—hup 2-3-4——— (*As Martha intones, Polly marches into the bedroom, with the blanket and the rifle. Martha crosses to behind couch to join Don. They stand, hands folded solemnly in front, looking down at Deerfield on the couch.*) What a waste of good liquor.

DON. Martha, I know it's hard to believe, but you're looking at the man who's going to break up my happy home.

MARTHA. Not in that condition, he won't.

DON. Everything he said tonight about my plays was true.

MARTHA. So what's the solution?

DON. I don't know yet. Maybe Penelope.

MARTHA. Penelope? Who her?

DON. The fourth side of the triangle. (*Leaning over couch.*) Penelope phoned.

DEERFIELD. (*Without opening his eyes.*) Penelope?

MARTHA. It talked!

DEERFIELD. What did you tell her?

DON. Sit up first.

DEERFIELD. I am sitting up.

MARTHA. Then we must be lying down. (*Don bends over couch and brings Deerfield to a sitting position. Deerfield's feet stiffly come to rest on the coffee table. His eyes remain closed. Martha crosses D. L. with her drink.*) He looked better the other way. (*Polly enters from bedroom. She has put on a robe, fixed her hair and tied a gay ribbon in it. She carries a robe for Don. She closes bedroom door.*)

POLLY. Good morning! How about some coffee?

DON. (*Glaring.*) See what I mean! She never put a ribbon in her hair for me at two in the morning.

POLLY. You never wrote a play for me.

DON. (*To Martha.*) Don't ever get married.

MARTHA. (*Crosses to hassock D. L., sits.*) Yes, it must be miserable to have someone around to talk to. (*To Polly.*) I'd love some coffee.

POLLY. (*At R. of couch, bending near Deerfield.*) How about you? (*He opens his eyes slowly, sees Polly directly before him.*)

DEERFIELD. Melinda! Are we alone?

DON. (*Coming to* R. *of Polly, and pulling her away.*) As alone as you two are ever going to be.

POLLY. (*To Deerfield.*) I'm going to heat up some coffee. You'll be as good as new in a few minutes. (*Crosses to kitchen door, patting Martha on the head as she passes. She exits into kitchen.*)

MARTHA. (*Reacting to the gentle pat.*) I should never drink on an empty head.

DEERFIELD. (*Straining his eyes to focus, beckoning to Martha.*) Would you mind coming a little closer?

MARTHA. (*Moving to couch, sits next to Deerfield.*) What have I got to lose?

DEERFIELD. (*Staring at Martha, with sudden recognition.*) Mother!

MARTHA. Mother?

DON. How's Dad?

DEERFIELD. (*Turning his head to focus on Don.*) Oh, it's you, Mr. Emerson. I wasn't supposed to see your wife again until to-morrow. My apologies.

DON. No apology necessary. Why waste a night, I always say.

MARTHA. I hate to change the subject, but who's Penelope?

DEERFIELD. The only girl in the world who thinks I'm irresistible. She's the one from Vassar who wears glasses.

MARTHA. Now I'd know her anywhere.

DON. She was relieved to hear you didn't make the grade with my stage-struck bride.

DEERFIELD. The night is young, Mr. Emerson.

MARTHA. And I'm so beautiful! (*Deerfield puts his head in Martha's lap.*)

DON. Martha, what's it worth for you to take him home?

MARTHA. His or mine? The rates vary.   (*Polly enters from the kitchen with a tray of cups.*)

POLLY. Here are the cups, everybody. Hot coffee in a minute. (*Puts tray on telephone ledge,* L.)

DON. I can't wait to pour it over him.

DEERFIELD. (*Recumbent.*) Coffee? Why don't we all get tight, as long as Mother's here?

MARTHA. (*To Polly.*) That's me.

POLLY. How do you feel, Deerfield?

33

DEERFIELD. (*Snapping his fingers.*) Like dancing. Is it too late to play records and dance?

MARTHA. It's never too late for your mother. How's your tango?

DON. I'm sure it's fine if you lead. I'll put on the records. (*Don crosses to phonograph, as Deerfield and Martha rise, and commence an elephantine tango from the couch to R. C., humming and swaying.*)

POLLY. Don! At this hour?

DON. Why not? All it will do is wake up the neighbors.

POLLY. Now stop it, Don. We don't even know who they are.

DON. This might bring us closer together. (*There is a sharp knock at the front door.*)

MARTHA. If that's the neighbors, they're very quick.

GLORIA. (O. S. *from hallway, knocking.*) Polly darling, are you up? Polly!

DON. You didn't tell me you were holding open house.

POLLY. It sounds like someone who knows me, doesn't it?

MARTHA. Be easy to find out by opening the door.

GLORIA. (O. S. *from hallway.*) Yoohoo, Polly! It's me, Gloria.

MARTHA. It's Gloria!

DON. (*To Martha, moving D. R. in front of fireplace.*) Who the hell is Gloria? (*Martha stands at the R. of Deerfield, who has collapsed on the hassock, R. C., his eyes closed.*)

MARTHA. Get up, Junior, we've got company. (*Polly goes up L. steps, crosses to front door and opens it. Gloria Martindale sweeps in, mink stole and all. She's a dazzling creature who's learned more about men in her twenty-eight years than Polly will in a hundred. She embraces Polly, her bejeweled arms holding two small overnight bags.*)

GLORIA. Polly, darling!

POLLY. (*Embracing her.*) This is a surprise! I didn't expect you until tomorrow.

DON. (*To Martha.*) I didn't expect her at all.

GLORIA. (*To Polly, who puts the bags down on the landing.*) Didn't your maid give you the message? I phoned this afternoon. From Chicago.

POLLY. I didn't even get any local messages. Come on, Gloria, I want you to meet everybody. (*Polly brings Gloria down C. steps.*) This is my husband, Don. This is Gloria. We grew up next door to each other in Akron.

34

GLORIA. Hi!

DON. Hi! Just passing through town?

POLLY. Gloria wrote me a month ago she was coming to New York to try her luck after the divorce. I'm sure I told you about her letter.

DON. When?

POLLY. While you were taking a shower.

DON. When else?

POLLY. And this is Deerfield Prescott. He wrote my new show.

GLORIA. Doesn't he ever open his eyes?

DON. We think he's much more fascinating this way. (*Martha has sidled up to Gloria. She picks up one end of the mink stole and blows on the fur, then drops the mink, satisfied.*)

GLORIA. (*To Martha.*) Who are you?

MARTHA. (*Pointing at the top of Deerfield's head.*) Mother. His.

POLLY. Don't be silly. This is Martha. She types all of Don's plays.

MARTHA. With these hot little fingers.

GLORIA. (*To Polly.*) You didn't write me you knew such interesting people.

MARTHA. Oh, we're just home folk. (*Martha executes a weary, wiggling tango through c., and collapses over the R. arm of the couch, lying flat on her back.*)

DEERFIELD. (*His eyes still closed.*) Maybe you are, but I'm not. My father has ten million, and three more the government doesn't know anything about.

GLORIA. (*Brightening, and taking a step nearer Deerfield.*) Well!

DON. (*To Gloria.*) Oh, don't waste your time on him. He's got his beady little eyes on Polly.

GLORIA. (*To Polly.*) Has he really?

POLLY. (*Posing.*) He knows what he wants when he wants it— and he wants me.

GLORIA. Isn't he a little young for you?

DON. (*Sits d. R. fireplace bench.*) She's going to age him.

GLORIA. (*To Polly.*) Now I'm sure I'll accept your invitation. Do you really have room for me?

POLLY. Sure we have.

DON. Sure we have. The secret room.

POLLY. (*Sweetly.*) Shut up, darling. (*To Gloria.*) Are those all your bags?

GLORIA. No, the rest are in the taxi. Don, would you get them like a nice fellow?

POLLY. Of course, he will. Won't you, dear?

DON. I have a feeling if I go out in the street, I won't get back in again.

POLLY. (*Crossing to Don.*) No one's going to lock you out. Just put Martha and Deerfield in the taxi and take Gloria's bags out.

DON. If your mother had only been firm about not letting you marry me! (*Don rises, crosses to R. of Deerfield, passes his hand in front of Deerfield's closed eyes. He calls to Martha.*) Oh—Mom!

MARTHA. (*Struggling to her feet.*) I'll go quietly. (*Crossing R. C., speaks to Gloria.*) Well, it's been awfully nice meeting you. (*She gathers up her shoes, hat, purse from R. chair. To Don.*) What do you want me to do with him? (*Coming to L. of Deerfield.*)

DON. Nothing he'll hate himself for in the morning.

MARTHA. (*Helping Don to get Deerfield to his feet.*) Watch it. Either he tilts a little, or I do. (*Don and Martha wheel Deerfield toward the C. steps, and start to take him out. His arms are across their shoulders. When he comes to the steps, he treads air, his full weight on Don and Martha. Martha's free hand goes to the small of her back.*) Oh—your mother's aching back! (*They go out, leaving the door open. Polly turns to Gloria.*)

POLLY. Let me look at you. (*Gloria pirouettes. Suddenly, there is a crash in the hall. They turn, startled. After a moment, Deerfield appears in the doorway, carrying Martha's hat.*)

DEERFIELD. Mother fell down. (*He exits. Gloria sits on fireplace bench, D. R., takes cigarette from purse and lights it. Polly sits across from her, on chair at table.*)

POLLY. Imagine! It's ten years since we've seen each other.

GLORIA. A lot of husbands have gone under the bridge since then. Don's your first, isn't he?

POLLY. And last.

GLORIA. You're as naive as ever. What about the playwright with the rich father? Where does he fit in?

POLLY. I'm not sure yet.

GLORIA. (*Intrigued.*) Then there is something going on. Tell me about it.

POLLY. Well, it all began this afternoon when I went to an audition. The next thing I knew Deerfield said he was madly in love with me —— (*She stops abruptly when Don appears in the doorway. He staggers under the weight of three pieces of luggage.*)

DON. Well, here I am again! Miami was wonderful. (*He sets the bags down on platform.*)

POLLY. Just put them in the bedroom, darling. (*Indicating the two smaller bags.*) Along with those others.

DON. (*Struggling to carry all the bags at once.*) It's lucky for me that you travel light. How the hell do the bellhops do it so easily? (*He finally gets all the bags under control, and starts down R. steps toward bedroom door.*)

POLLY. (*Shivering.*) Close the door, darling. (*Don shoots Polly a murderous glance. He manages to get back onto the landing. He kicks the front door shut. He starts down the R. steps again.*)

DON. Can you think of anything else you want me to do—while I've got both hands free?

POLLY. No, thank you.

DON. (*Staggering into the bedroom with the luggage.*) I may be ruptured for life!

POLLY. Bring the electric blanket back with you, darling. I'll make up the couch for you. (*There is a sudden crash in the bedroom. Don re-appears, carrying only two bags.*)

DON. The couch?

POLLY. The one you always sleep on when we have guests.

DON. (*Indicating couch.*) Oh, *that* couch.

POLLY. (*To Gloria, ignoring Don.*) You look wonderful for someone who just got divorced.

DON. Yes, you do! You really do! (*Exits into bedroom with luggage.*)

GLORIA. He doesn't like me, does he?

POLLY. He doesn't like anybody tonight. (*Rises, starts for the couch.*) I'd better make up the couch.

GLORIA. (*Following.*) Wait. I'll help you. (*Gloria stops C., looks for a place to douse her cigarette. At this moment, Don enters from the bedroom with the electric blanket. He rushes to Gloria's assistance with great politeness, bringing her an ash tray from the R. table.*)

DON. Oh, let me! (*He douses the cigarette, elaborately.*)

GLORIA. Thanks. You can be sweet.

DON. Not if I try. (*Hands blanket to Gloria, crosses* D. R. *with ash tray and puts it back on* R. *table.*)

POLLY. (*Behind couch.*) I'll have the couch made up in a minute.

GLORIA. (*Crouching at* R. *end of couch.*) I'll take care of this end, Polly. (*The girls spread the blanket, tuck it in.*) I think this is the first time I've made a bed since we went to Girl Scout camp.

DON. (*Moving above couch, holds up hand in Scout formation.*) I'm honored.

POLLY. Don loves to sleep on this couch. He even prefers it to a double bed.

GLORIA. Not me.

DON. Not me, either.

GLORIA. (*Rising, turning* C.) I love what you've done with this old brownstone.

DON. To say nothing of what she's done with me.

POLLY. (*Patting couch—from* L. *end.*) See how simple it is, darling. Your feet will stay under nice and comfy.

DON. (*Patting pillow.*) And my broken neck goes right here! Doesn't it?

POLLY. You'll sleep like a log. (*Don starts to take off his robe.*) Don! Gloria's here.

DON. (*Wrapping and tying the robe with great ado.*) Sorry. I lost my head. (*Moves* R. *around couch, to below couch.*)

GLORIA. Well, I'll say good night. (*Goes toward bedroom.*)

POLLY. (L. *of couch.*) Good night, Gloria. I'll be with you as soon as I put him to bed. Say good night to Gloria, Don.

DON. Good night to Gloria. (*Gloria exits into bedroom. Polly hits the light switch* D. L., *and all the lights go out except the lamp on ledge over* L. *end of couch. Tossing his robe on the* D. L. *hassock.*) While you're at it, you'd better turn out the coffee. It'll be boiled out before morning. (*Polly goes into the kitchen. Don settles on the couch.*)

POLLY. (*As she goes.*) Gloria's nice, isn't she?

DON. She's a cobra. I hope her husband recovers. Will you please tell me why you're bringing all these strangers into our lives? (*The kitchen light goes out, and Polly returns, and moves above the couch.*)

POLLY. I've known Gloria longer than I've known you. She needs a shoulder to cry on, after what she's been through.

DON. After *who* she's been through. Why does she have to spend

38

the night here? Don't tell me every hotel in New York is off limits for her.

POLLY. When your college roommate was here, didn't he stay with us?

DON. He took the couch, not my bedroom. And he was in uniform on a three-day pass.

POLLY. I'm sure Gloria doesn't plan to stay any longer than that.

DON. (*After long look at bedroom.*) Okay, plug me in and set me for 72 degrees. (*Polly plugs in the cord behind the couch.*) You know, I think that'll be the title of my next play: "I Married an Electric Blanket."

POLLY. (*Leaning over him.*) I don't know why I love you, but I do. Now?

DON. (*Lying back, serenely.*) Now what?

POLLY. My good night kiss. The one I didn't give Deerfield.

DON. Okay, but only to avoid a scene. (*They kiss, without an embrace.*) He didn't miss a thing.

POLLY. It takes two to make a kiss. (*Turns off lamp over couch.*) Sleep tight. (*She starts for the bedroom, by way of front door, going up L. steps.*)

DON. If you get lonesome in the middle of the night—(*Pats couch.*) be my guest. (*Polly pauses at the front door, slips the safety chain into place. Then she turns, and hurries down R. steps into bedroom. She closes the door.*)

POLLY. Am I glad you're here, Gloria!

GLORIA. (o. s. *from bedroom.*) Am I glad to be here! (*The girls giggle wildly. Don huddles under blanket.*) Now, give me all the dirt.

POLLY. Well, to begin with, Don insists I'm going to be unfaithful to him. (*Don pushes his head out from under blanket, listens.*)

GLORIA. Unfaithful to him? Well, are you? (o. s., *there is complete silence. Don sits up. He gets off the couch and darts to the bedroom door. He puts his ear against the louvred top section.*)

POLLY. (o. s.) I really don't know what to do. Don is always so right about everything —— (*Closes top louvres. Don drops to his knees, puts ear against bottom section of louvres.*) And he gets so angry when I prove he's wrong. It seems to me —— (*Closes bottom section of louvres, leaving Don in the dark silence.*)

CURTAIN

ACT II

SCENE 1

*The same, except that a small piano now stands at the L.
of the dining table. A crumpled pillow, the electric
blanket and sheets are on the couch. Before the curtain
rises, someone can be heard at the piano, playing "L'il
Ol' You and L'il Ol' Me." Several letters are on the
phonograph. The curtains are open. Polly's purse is on
the bench by the front door. The chair that was formerly
U. L. on the platform has been moved D. L. against the
wall. On the dining table are Don's and Deerfield's briefcases, typed MS papers, and the typewriter. MS sheets of
music are on the piano. Deerfield's coat hangs on chair R.
of dining table.*

*It is morning, several weeks later. Don, in pajamas and
robe, sits on R. end of dining table, typing his playscript.
Deerfield, his tie open, and his sleeves rolled up, is at the
piano. He starts to sing the song. When Deerfield com-
mences to vocalize, Don glowers. When Deerfield swings
into tempo, Don helplessly slips into a similar rhythm at
the typewriter. Don is further disconcerted when Deerfield spreads his composition sheets across the table right
onto Don's typing. Don folds the sheets back into place.*

DEERFIELD. If I'm in the way here—(*Indicating coffee table by
couch.*) why don't you work down there?
DON. In my bedroom?
DEERFIELD. You don't like having me around any more than
you do Gloria, do you? (*Don picks up his typewriter and comes
down* C. *steps, taking machine and MS to coffee table.*) Do you?
DON. It's a moot question. I'd have to think about it. (*He sits
on couch and starts to type again, but Deerfield continues to sing
the lyrics and Don again finds himself typing in the rhythm as
Deerfield sings the phrase over and over. Don waves desperately
for attention.*) Okay, okay! Hold it! (*As Deerfield turns.*) The
tempo was fine before. You can skip the words.

40

DEERFIELD. Don't you like them?

DON. Why don't you write a nice lyric like, "Thanks for the use of your piano, and I'll stop looking calf-eyed at your wife"?

DEERFIELD. Doesn't rhyme. Besides, I think she's getting used to having me around.

DON. After only three weeks? I had a feeling it would take much longer than that. My spies tell me you haven't been making much progress with Polly. What seems to be the trouble?

DEERFIELD. (*Rises, crosses to above* c. *of railing.*) She won't co-operate. She keeps telling me she's crazy about you.

DON. You going to believe her or that song you wrote for her?

DEERFIELD. (*Sits on edge of dining table.*) The song, but a fellow can only do so much love-making on paper.

DON. Depends if you want to create or procreate.

DEERFIELD. Maybe I'm just impatient.

DON. (*Rises, crosses to below rail,* R. *of Deerfield.*) No, it's more than that. You've gone into the wrong racket. Wife-*stealing*. It's a lost art. The popular fad these days is wife-*borrowing*.

DEERFIELD. (*Returning to piano.*) That sounds highly immoral to me. I was brought up very strict. New England, you know. (*Sits at piano.*)

DON. (*Going up* c. *steps to landing.*) I don't know anything except that I'd like to get into the bathroom and shave and shower. What happened to my morning paper?

DEERFIELD. I haven't seen it.

DON. (*Crosses down* R. *steps to phonograph cabinet.*) Ah, the mail . . .

DEERFIELD. Anything for me today?

DON. (*Sorting mail.*) Deerfield, Gloria, Gloria, Deerfield, Gloria. A postcard for me! Now how did that get in there? (*Don shoves Gloria's letters through the louvres of the bedroom door, then crosses to the piano with Deerfield's mail.*) Tell me, Deerfield, now that we've learned to live with each other, what do you see in my wife?

DEERFIELD. (*Turns to Don.*) Do you really want to know?

DON. (*Crossing above table to Deerfield.*) Since you're the last person in the world I'd choose to sit around with on a desert island and chit-chat, I really want to know.

DEERFIELD. All right. I'll tell you exactly what I see in your wife. My mother. Before she married my father.

41

DON. You must have made a lovely flower boy at the wedding.

DEERFIELD. I wasn't even born then.

DON. I know. I know.

DEERFIELD. But I've seen pictures of her. You may not believe it, but I'm very self-analytical. I have to be until I can afford a psychiatrist. (*Deerfield leans wistfully on one elbow at the piano. Juliet enters from the kitchen, carrying a tray with a sandwich and a glass of milk, for Deerfield. She moves up L. steps to above L. end of table.*)

JULIET. (*To Don.*) You still here?

DON. (*Crossing R. on platform.*) There's a traffic jam in the bedroom.

JULIET. Want me to make up your bed?

DON. Oh, serve our guest first. I'm only the man who pays for you and the other utilities. (*Deerfield plays his song.*)

JULIET. (*To Don.*) Did I remember to talk to you about a raise?

DON. You can play louder now, Deerfield.

JULIET. (*Indicating tray.*) There's the nourishment for your ulcer. (*Dubiously.*) Are you sure you're supposed to have peanut butter and salami?

DEERFIELD. One kills the other.

JULIET. (*To Don, who is looking in the mirror on partition wall.*) How about you, Mr. Emerson? Will you want breakfast this morning?

DON. (*Crossing down C. steps to the couch.*) You sound like you've already chopped up the ground glass to put into it. I'll just have a cup of coffee.

JULIET. (*Crossing to top of bannister, R., looking at watch.*) Shouldn't you be at work?

DON. (*Between his teeth, desperately.*) I'm trying to get into the bathroom. (*The phone rings on ledge L. and Don and Deerfield move for it, simultaneously.*) Do you mind? It's still listed in my name.

DEERFIELD. Sorry. I sort of feel this is my home away from home. (*Returns to piano, sits.*)

DON. Not for much longer. (*Into phone.*) Hello. . . . Yes, he's here. (*Offering phone to Deerfield.*) It's for you. (*Deerfield comes to rail at L. steps. Don presses the phone into his hand with an avuncular pat.*) A girl. Now, don't get rattled. Act like it happens to you every day.

DEERFIELD. (*Into phone.*) Hello. Deerfield Prescott on this end. . . . Oh, hello. (*To Don.*) It's only Penelope. She wants to know what's new.

DON. (*Crossing behind couch to planter,* R.) Tell her there's plenty new. I've decided the piano goes back to the piano rental people, Gloria packs up bag and luggage, and you go back under your rock.

DEERFIELD. (*Turns back, sits on rail, talks into phone.*) I'm being dispossessed. (*Juliet crosses down* C. *steps to behind couch, and strips off the bedclothes.*)

JULIET. (*To Don.*) You're making an awful lot of decisions on your own. Have you cleared all this with Mrs. Emerson?

DON. I've slept on her mother's couch for the last time. (*Indicating bedroom.*) You going into the girls' dormitory?

JULIET. I could be coaxed.

DON. (*As Juliet goes to bedroom with wad of bedclothes.*) Kindly tell the present Mrs. Emerson and the future Mrs. Prescott that our arrangement calls for her and her poison pen pal from Akron to be out of my way by 9:30 every morning. It's nearly ten now.

JULIET. Yes, sir. (*She exits into bedroom with bedclothes.*)

DEERFIELD. (*Into phone.*) That's not funny, Penelope. Goodbye. (*Hangs up.*)

DON. What's not funny?

DEERFIELD. She wants to take me out tonight and ply me with wine.

DON. Well, why don't you be smart and settle for her, or somebody else your own age?

DEERFIELD. Girls my age despise boys their age. Except Penelope. And actually she's two years younger than I am, but on account of girls maturing faster than boys, she's about five years older.

DON. (*Goes to couch, sits.*) At that rate, you'll never catch up with her. Do your parents approve of Penelope?

DEERFIELD. They don't even know she exists.

DON. Do you? I mean, have you ever made a pass at her?

DEERFIELD. No, but I've thought of it.

DON. It isn't exactly the same thing. (*Picks up play script from coffee table.*) Tell me, Deerfield, as one playwright to another, how do you like the new title of my play instead of "Without Passion"?

DEERFIELD. What is it?

DON. "Positively Without Passion." How do you like it?

DEERFIELD. It's longer.

DON. So's the play. I added a new scene.

DEERFIELD. That's good.

DON. Don't you want to know what it is?

DEERFIELD. Sure, if you promise not to ask me how I like it. I seem to remember that led to some trouble the last time.

DON. When a writer asks you how you like his play, you're supposed to tell him just that, not dissect it. Anyhow, I have this happen in the third act. The father explains to his son that because of a psychological trauma he hasn't slept with his wife— the boy's mother—for twenty years.

DEERFIELD. How old is the son?

DON. Nineteen. That's when the father suddenly realizes that the boy, whom he never could stand, isn't his. He finds out he's been hating a stranger all those years and it takes a big load off his mind. What do you think?

DEERFIELD. (*Rises, comes down* L. *steps and moves behind couch.*) It's pretty strong stuff for a musical.

DON. (*Rises and follows.*) Musical? You're being deliberately evasive. You know damn well my play isn't a musical. Give me an honest answer.

DEERFIELD. I like it.

DON. (*Turning away, to* R. *of couch.*) What the hell do you know? I can tell by your attitude you think it stinks.

DEERFIELD. (*Crosses to below* L. *end of couch.*) No, really, I do like it. It's over my head, but I like it.

DON. (*Drops script on coffee table as they meet below couch.*) Well, I'll tell you something. I don't care how much you like it. All I want from you is to keep your mind and your hands off my enchanted wife, to get your musical opened in New Haven and closed in New York, and then vanish from my life as mysteriously as you entered it.

DEERFIELD. If you're annoyed about sharing your typewriter with me ——

DON. Annoyed? I'm honored. Who do you think goaded me into rewriting my play? *You.* I'll admit it. You were a challenge. And if a certain something happens in a little while, I will have met that challenge.

44

DEERFIELD. I'm still in the dark.

DON. Just don't be surprised if my play goes on before they can even sew the Confederate flags for your show. I told you not to make so many changes.

DEERFIELD. I had to. The people who are putting up the money come from Atlanta, so they want the South to win the Civil War.

DON. That's one way to make history. Do you still free the slaves?

DEERFIELD. Yes, but only as a dream sequence. (*Polly enters from bedroom, dressed to go out. She carries purse. She goes up R. steps to platform to get purse from bench by front door.*)

POLLY. (*To Don.*) Good morning, darling. Haven't you gone to work yet?

DON. (*Turning to Polly.*) The agency has a firm rule against employees coming to work in their pajamas. (*Indicating bedroom.*) All my clothes happen to be in there. (*Gloria enters from bedroom in Polly's robe and slippers. She carries the New York Times.*)

POLLY. (*To Gloria.*) Aren't we thoughtless?

GLORIA. (*Behind R. chair, stretching luxuriously.*) Good morning!

DON. (*To Gloria.*) How do you manage to get by with only ten hours' sleep? Oh, that's where my morning paper went, of course. (*Takes paper from her.*)

GLORIA. Sorry.

DEERFIELD. (*Meets Don at C.*) Could I see how my father's stocks are doing?

DON. By all means. Shall I turn it to the right page for you? (*Turns pages of paper, hands it to Deerfield.*) Mrs. Emerson, could I talk to you alone for one minute?

POLLY. (*Coming down C. steps to R. of Don.*) Of course. Go ahead and talk.

DON. Alone means just the two of us. We don't need the gay divorcee or the poor man's Cole Porter.

GLORIA. (*Crossing below through C. toward kitchen.*) Come on, Deerfield. We've been banished. You can watch me cook my own breakfast. (*Exits into kitchen.*)

DEERFIELD. (*Following.*) Sure. I find something most appealing about watching a woman bend over a hot stove. (*Exits into kitchen. Polly sits on* C. *bassock and changes contents of one purse into another purse.*)

POLLY. Now, what did you want to talk about, Don? I've got an appointment.

DON. (*Taking stage,* R. C.) I've made up my mind. I've decided to change our lives back to the way they were before this apartment became a boarding house and a rehearsal hall. The piano's going out, and Deerfield with it. Now, what about Gloria?

POLLY. Not so loud. She can hear you.

DON. I hope so. When does she plan to move out?

POLLY. (*Rising, goes to Don.*) Any day now. Honestly, Don, I didn't know she was going to stay this long.

DON. (*Crosses to* C. *bassock, sits.*) I did. When I carried in those five bags full of her armor and war paint. She's done only one considerate thing in all the time she's been here. Spending that weekend in Westchester. (*Polly smiles reminiscently, and moves up against Don's shoulder.*)

POLLY. It was nice.

DON. You don't suppose we could find her some weekend friends out on Fire Island?

POLLY. If you feel that frustrated, we could check into a hotel.

DON. As man and wife?

POLLY. It sounds exciting. Why don't we try it sometime?

DON. Just don't make the same offer to Deerfield.

POLLY. You and your theories about married women playing around. See how wrong you were about him and me?

DON. How do I know I was? The husband's always the last one to find out. It's traditional.

POLLY. (*Sits on Don's lap, kisses him.*) Want to meet me later? You can skip lunch and we can check in at the Waldorf. Under assumed names if you want to.

DON. No, thanks, but until we meet again under our own roof —— (*Kisses her affectionately. The front door opens, and Martha enters. Don and Polly break. She goes to couch, sits. He crosses upstage into corner of bannister,* L. *of* C. *steps.*)

MARTHA. Don't mind me. I love a nice domestic scene.

DON. What are you doing in this neighborhood? I said I'd call you if I had any revisions that needed typing.

MARTHA. (*Getting umbrella from stand by front door.*) I forgot my umbrella.

POLLY. Do you want to stay for lunch?

MARTHA. No, thanks. (*Comes down onto second* c. *step.*) I promised to make an appearance at Mahoney's. They're dedicating a bar stool to me. With an engraved silver nameplate reading, "Martha Sat Here."

DON. I hear Schenley's paid for the whole thing.

POLLY. I don't know how you do it.

MARTHA. It isn't easy. (*Goes up to platform.*) I'll check in later to see if there's any work for me. Where's Deerfield? (*To Polly.*) Did he give up on you?

DON. If he's going to get anywhere with Polly, he'll have to do it today. I put him on a deadline.

POLLY. (*Teasing.*) I may never know what I'm missing. (*Martha goes to the front door, opens it.*)

MARTHA. That's the excuse I always gave myself. Well, pick it up where you left off. (*She exits.*)

DON. I'd love to, but I better get dressed. (*He gives Polly a wolf growl, and starts for the bedroom, as Juliet enters from bedroom.*)

JULIET. (*Goes to Don, curtsies.*) I've drawn your tub, sire.

DON. Scalding hot, I'm sure. (*He crosses below Juliet, goes to bedroom.*)

JULIET. (*Calling after him.*) Oh, Gloria used up all the "His" towels. Can you use one marked "Hers"?

DON. I'll force myself. (*Exits into bedroom.*)

POLLY. Juliet dear, is it too late for a little breakfast?

JULIET. (*Crossing to kitchen door.*) This is the only cafeteria in town that never closes. (*As Juliet is almost at the kitchen door, it bursts open and Deerfield enters, almost conking Juliet with the door. She leaps back.*)

DEERFIELD. Sorry. (*Juliet spies Gloria through the open door.*)

JULIET. (*Charging out through the kitchen door.*) What are you doing with my stove? (*Deerfield closes kitchen door after Juliet.*)

POLLY. What were you playing before?

DEERFIELD. "Li'l Ol' You and Li'l Ol' Me." Will you have time to run over a chorus before you go out?

POLLY. (*Circling* R. *side of room, searchingly.*) If it doesn't take me too long to find my gloves. You haven't seen them, have you?

DEERFIELD. No.

POLLY. One left and one right. Maybe Juliet knows where they are. Be right back. (*Exits into kitchen. Deerfield looks after her with love-sick eyes, then goes toward kitchen door.*)

DEERFIELD. (*Reading scene.*) "Melinda, is it really you?" . . . (*With Southern accent.*) "Yes, darling, they brought you here after the Battle of Bull Run. You've been in a coma for I don't know how many days." . . . "What are you doing in a nurse's uniform, Melinda?" . . . (*The kitchen door swings open wide, knocking Deerfield against the wall behind it, as Polly enters.*)

POLLY. (*Stepping into room.*) Deerfield, if you want to run over the new song now . . . (*She stops, mystified.*) Deerfield, where are you?

DEERFIELD. (*From behind the door.*) In a coma after the Battle of Bull Run. (*Polly swings the door back and discloses him nursing his head. His glasses are cockeyed across his face.*)

POLLY. Oh, I'm sorry. (*Straightening his glasses.*) Did I hurt you?

DEERFIELD. Only by your attitude. (*Emotionally.*) Polly, this is the closest we've ever been together. (*Puts his arms tentatively on her shoulders.*) Would you mind?

POLLY. Would I mind what?

DEERFIELD. I don't know. This is as far as I've ever gone with anybody. (*Sniffing.*) What have you got on?

POLLY. Oh, this is Gloria's. You like it?

DEERFIELD. No, I mean your perfume. It's doing something to me.

POLLY. It's called "Easy, Boy." Now, play your song. I'm already late for my appointment.

DEERFIELD. (*Going up L. steps to piano.*) It's only thirty-two bars. (*He hands Polly the song.*)

POLLY. All right. Just one quick chorus. (*Deerfield starts to play, Polly starts to sing.*)

DEERFIELD. Wait till I find the right key. (*He starts her off.*) That's fine. (*In the lyrics, on "Juniper tree," Deerfield crosses down L. steps to the couch and lies down, head R.*)

POLLY. Where are you going? What are you doing?

DEERFIELD. Keep on singing. I want to find out how the scene feels. This is a hospital bed, and I'm Jeff, lying here after the battle.

POLLY. Are you badly wounded?

DEERFIELD. I haven't decided yet. Go ahead and finish the song.

48

(*Polly sings a chorus, doing part of it while pirouetting around the room, up and down the* C. *and* R. *steps, and finishing on couch beside Deerfield.*) Now you kiss me.

POLLY. With Don in the bedroom?

DEERFIELD. I mean you kiss Jeff. Tenderly.

POLLY. I like the song. I think it's cute.

DEERFIELD.You're breaking the mood.

POLLY. I know.

DEERFIELD. Kiss me, and then I'll sing the last eight bars. (*Polly kisses him on the cheek. They resume singing, in brighter tempo, as Deerfield indicates the beat by rapping on the coffee table. Juliet enters from the kitchen with Polly's gloves, and carrying a small watering can. She stares at the two on the couch.*)

JULIET. (*As they hold the last note.*) And li'l ol' me! (*Polly and Deerfield turn, startled. He tries to sit up, but Polly pushes him back.*)

POLLY. Lie down and stop looking so guilty. (*To Juliet.*) It isn't what you think at all.

JULIET. It's a darned good imitation. I found your gloves. They were in the bread box again.

POLLY. We were merely rehearsing a scene in the hospital.

JULIET. (*Crossing to planter,* U. R.) That's where he'll be if Mr. Emerson ever finds out.

POLLY. (*Rising, goes to Juliet.*) Juliet, you didn't see anything because there was nothing to see. We were running over a song at the piano when you walked in. Do you understand?

JULIET. No.

POLLY. Do you really think that green silk dress of mine will fit you if you shorten it a little?

JULIET. I understand. If you throw in the hat that matches.

POLLY. You'll look ridiculous, but it's yours. (*To Deerfield, handing him the song.*) Rehearsal is over. Here's your music, and there's the piano. Be brilliant some more.

DEERFIELD. (*Rising.*) Polly, didn't that kiss do anything to you?

POLLY. What kiss?

JULIET. What kiss?

POLLY. See? (*Goes up* C. *steps to front door.*)

JULIET. Where are you going?

POLLY. Big secret. (*Gloria enters from kitchen, sees Polly at door.*)

GLORIA. Polly, aren't we going shopping like we planned?

POLLY. Sure. I'll be back in a little while. (*To Juliet.*) Oh, and never mind about breakfast.

JULIET. I'd already forgotten about it.

POLLY. 'Bye now. (*Exits.*)

DEERFIELD. I hope she hurries back. I'm in the mood for anything but work.

JULIET. I knew I put too much peanut butter in that sandwich. (*To Gloria, who crosses R.*) May I ask what you're doing in Mrs. Emerson's robe and slippers?

GLORIA. Oh, we've worn each other's clothes ever since we were kids. (*Observes Juliet watering at planter.*) How's your garden coming along? (*Turns D. S., leans over R. table for cigarette.*)

JULIET. (*Her head close to the plants.*) I don't know how *snails* get in here. (*Deerfield bends over his music at coffee table. Bedroom door opens and Don enters, dressed in street clothes.*)

DON. Ah, the three witches! (*Goes up L. steps on platform.*) What are you plotting? (*To Juliet.*) You look especially guilty.

JULIET. Me? I was just thinking of a new matching outfit somebody gave me.

GLORIA. (*To Juliet.*) Did you iron Polly's scarves yet? I washed my hair this morning.

JULIET. In the third drawer.

GLORIA. Thanks. (*She exits into bedroom.*)

DON. She uses more hot water than Old Faithful.

JULIET. (*Busy with her plants.*) Me and my green thumbs!

DON. I still haven't had my coffee.

JULIET. (*Marching into the kitchen.*) If I didn't want to see how this works out, I would have quit weeks ago! (*Exits.*)

DEERFIELD. Well, I'm sure glad things are working out for you, Mr. Emerson.

DON. I'm sorry I can't say as much for you.

DEERFIELD. I still have the rest of the day. If you meant what you said about my working elsewhere.

DON. I meant it. (*Looking at watch.*) Tell Juliet I'll skip the coffee. What happened to my morning paper?

DEERFIELD. (*Goes up C. steps and joins Don by the front door.*) I thought you were all through with it.

DON. (*With sarcasm.*) I guess I am.

50

DEERFIELD. Do you really hate me, Mr. Emerson? As much as my father does?

DON. I'm sure he doesn't hate you. You probably just bewilder him.

DEERFIELD. No more than he does me. Maybe I'm like the son in your play.

DON. The son in my play?

DEERFIELD. I'm going to catch my mother in a good mood and ask her if I'm a bastard.

DON. I don't think there's any doubt. (*Exits through front door. Juliet enters from kitchen with a cup of coffee on a tray, just as Gloria enters from bedroom.*)

GLORIA. (*Meeting Juliet below* C. *steps.*) Oh, thanks, Juliet. I feel like another cup of coffee.

JULIET. This is for Mr. Emerson and it's the last cup.

DEERFIELD. (*Moving* L. *on platform to above dining table.*) He left.

GLORIA. Anyway, I like it black. Would it be too much bother to make some fresh?

JULIET. (*Heading for the kitchen again.*) Bother? What else have I got to do besides the laundry, the ironing and shop for dinner? This will keep the day from seeming long!

GLORIA. I made the bed this morning.

JULIET. That's a big help. Today's the day I change the sheets. (*Exits, kitchen.*)

GLORIA. (*Sits chair* R., *lights cigarette.*) Well, how are you doing, Deerfield?

DEERFIELD. Fine. I'll have the second act rewritten by the end of the week.

GLORIA. No, I mean with Polly. You making any progress?

DEERFIELD. (*Discouraged.*) Progress? It's nearly three weeks since I met her, and our affair is still purely platonic.

GLORIA. What are you waiting for?

DEERFIELD. It's all Don's fault. He made Polly promise she wouldn't see me anywhere but here and Sardi's. (*He sits on piano keys.*)

GLORIA. That's pretty. Is it from the show?

DEERFIELD. You're a woman of the world, Gloria. You've been around. Maybe you could figure out some way for me to get somewhere with Polly.

GLORIA. Have you got an older brother for me?

DEERFIELD. I'm an only child.

GLORIA. Forgive me, I should have known.

DEERFIELD. (*Crosses down* L. *steps above Gloria, to* R.) My father used to look at me and say, "I either should have had a lot more children, or one less."

GLORIA. How do you and he get along?

DEERFIELD. Wonderful, except when we're together. He doesn't understand my generation.

GLORIA. Who does?

DEERFIELD. (*Sits on fireplace bench,* R.) People don't realize how tough it is to be an overprivileged child. I had it worse than anyone.

GLORIA. In what way?

DEERFIELD. (*Lying on fireplace bench, head* D. S.) I was the only boy in the dormitory whose parents had never been divorced. That's tough on a fellow. It makes him feel left out of things.

GLORIA. Your folks certainly didn't do right by you.

DEERFIELD. I've lived all my life with the same parents. My roommate really got the breaks. He had three complete sets. How can you be exposed to life if you spend all your formative years with the same pair of adults? With so much security at home, I felt insecure when I had to face the outside world. Maybe that's why I'm not getting anywhere with Polly. I haven't any confidence.

GLORIA. (*Rises, crosses to couch.*) You haven't any technique and finesse. And that's what it takes to make love to a married woman. At your age it's mostly muscle.

DEERFIELD. (*Rising, follows Gloria.*) Did your husband have technique and finesse?

GLORIA. Which one?

DEERFIELD. I thought you were married only once.

GLORIA. Once for love, twice for money. I'm a three-time loser.

DEERFIELD. I'm sure you know your business, but can't youthful enthusiasm take the place of mature technique?

GLORIA. Deerfield, suppose I could manage to leave you here alone with Polly for a while. What would you do first?

DEERFIELD. Make sure Don was in his office.

GLORIA. Well, that's smart. I've got an idea. Come over here, Deerfield.

DEERFIELD. (*Hesitating.*) I really should finish that scene.

52

GLORIA. This one's more important. For the next five minutes, I want you to pretend that I'm Polly and you're you.

DEERFIELD. (*Going to the couch.*) Oh—a rehearsal! Gee, you're a darned good sport to let me rehearse what might never happen.

GLORIA. I just want to see if I've lost my touch. Sit down.

DEERFIELD. (*Sits on couch, crossing his legs.*) Now what do I do?

GLORIA. You might try holding my hands—putting your arms around me.

DEERFIELD. In the middle of the morning?

GLORIA. If there's anything I hate, it's a clock watcher.

DEERFIELD. What if someone walks in?

GLORIA. I'll deny anything they see. (*She turns Deerfield so he is facing properly.*) Oh, Deerfield, I'll just have to show you what I mean by technique and finesse. (*Cuddles against his shoulder, her legs tucked on the couch.*) Now, can you imagine that I'm Polly?

DEERFIELD. Say, you're surprisingly warm.

GLORIA. (*As he doesn't move.*) Well—what are you waiting for?

DEERFIELD. Suppose you get carried away?

GLORIA. You only live once. (*She lies in his lap, he folds his arms.*) Do you have to keep your glasses on?

DEERFIELD. I want to see what I'm doing.

GLORIA. It's better with your glasses off. (*Deerfield kisses her with passion. Gloria's arm goes around Deerfield's neck in an involuntary reflex. The front door opens, and Martha enters. Obviously, she has had a few drinks. She takes two tipsy steps, then stares in stark astonishment at what she sees. She turns back to look at the number on the open door to be sure she's in the right apartment. The pair on the couch are in such a position that even when they separate, Deerfield holds Gloria so that her face is not visible to Martha.*)

DEERFIELD. (*Commencing this line just before Martha enters.*) Polly, my sweet—(*Martha hears Polly's name.*) Polly, my darling —will you go away with me to a new world—to my apartment on East Sixty-third? (*Martha re-acts violently, a stricken hand on her solar plexus. She finds her way out, closing the door after her, as the embrace on the couch continues.*)

CURTAIN

53

ACT II

Scene 2

The same. Fifteen minutes later.

Deerfield sits on the couch, arms folded, looking very proud of himself. There is an insistent rapping at the front door. Martha enters when Deerfield goes up C. steps and moves to the door.

MARTHA. (*Carries purse which she puts on bench by front door along with hat.*) Hi!

DEERFIELD. Hi!

MARTHA. (*Shutting door and hanging hat on umbrella stand at door.*) Anything new?

DEERFIELD. No, same old routine.

MARTHA. Really? (*Indicating smear on his lips.*) What are you eating today besides lipstick?

DEERFIELD. Lipstick? (*Puts hand to mouth, looks at it.*) Now how do you suppose that got there?

MARTHA. You're the writer. (*Looks around.*) I see you did away with everybody.

DEERFIELD. Juliet's in the basement with the laundry. Gloria's taking a cold shower.

MARTHA. I won't ask about Polly. I'll just tell you this, Mr. Deerfield Prescott. About fifteen minutes ago I walked in and saw you on that couch in what the papers refer to as a compromising situation.

DEERFIELD. I thought I heard the door open and close, but I was busy at the time.

MARTHA. Deerfield, how could you?

DEERFIELD. It was easy, once I got the hang of it.

MARTHA. But in Don's own home. Take my advice, Deerfield. Be smart and get out of here before you get your jaw fractured.

DEERFIELD. (*Backing away.*) You're going to hit me?

MARTHA. No, Don is. After I walked in on you, I went back to

Mahoney's for another tranquilizer. Then I examined my conscience and decided I owed it to Don to tell him what you did.

DEERFIELD. Why would he be interested?

MARTHA. Why would he be interested! Anyway, I phoned Don and I said, "Take it easy, Don, be calm, don't get excited"—and then I told him exactly what I saw.

DEERFIELD. What did he say?

MARTHA. "I'm coming home and kill him in cold blood!" Take a powder, Deerfield. I don't want your cold blood on my hands. (*Pushing him* L. *along platform toward garden.*)

DEERFIELD. I can't go now. I have to finish the retreat from Vicksburg.

MARTHA. First finish the retreat from Seventy-fifth Street. (*Gathering up his papers on table and piano.*) Take the whole Civil War with you. Fort Sumter has been fired on. (*She starts to stuff the papers in one of the briefcases on the table.*)

DEERFIELD. (*Going to her.*) Careful! That's the only copy of my revisions.

MARTHA. (*Turning to piano.*) What about this sheet music? It might have your fingerprints on it. (*Drops music into briefcase.*)

DEERFIELD. I'm not going until I know what this is all about.

MARTHA. (*Stuffing sandwich and plate into briefcase.*) Do you want the rest of your salami? You may have to barricade yourself in your apartment until Don simmers down.

DEERFIELD. I'm not going to make a move until I talk to Polly.

MARTHA. You sure fooled me, sonny. (*Ruefully.*) Time was when I could spot a sex maniac at fifty paces.

DEERFIELD. My affection for Polly has nothing to do with sex.

MARTHA. You keep right on saying that to the men in the ambulance. (*She closes briefcase, pushes it into his arms, pushes him toward door, gathering up his coat from chair* R. *of table as they pass.*) That way lies freedom. (*Points out front door.*)

DEERFIELD. Are you trying to tell me to go?

MARTHA. That's my impression. (*Juliet enters from kitchen with fresh linen for bedroom.*)

JULIET. I thought I heard voices.

MARTHA. (*Desperately.*) One of them is going to be stilled forever if he doesn't get out.

JULIET. What's the problem?

MARTHA. They did and Don knows.

55

JULIET. (*Moving* C., *intrigued.*) No!

MARTHA. Yes!

JULIET. When did they have time?

MARTHA. How long does it take you to go down to the laundry, put in the clothes, start the machine ——

DEERFIELD. (*Crossing to* R. *of Martha.*) Wait a minute! Are you trying to say that Polly and I ——?

MARTHA. (*Interrupting.*) I sure am!

DEERFIELD. But she hasn't even been here.

MARTHA. That's doing it the hard way. (O. S., *in hall, doorslam, sound of running feet.*) The way he slammed that front door, he's furious! Juliet, put on the chain! (*Juliet runs up* C. *steps, puts the safety chain on the front door, and leans against the door.*)

DEERFIELD. But I can explain everything.

MARTHA. Not to a husband running a fever of 180. (*Don tries the front door, calls out from hall.*)

DON. Open up, somebody! (*Knocks.*)

MARTHA. You can still get away through the garden. The wall's only nine feet tall. A desperate man can make it.

DEERFIELD. I'm too yellow to run. (*Don's hand appears through the crack in the door. Juliet disengages Don's hand, closes door again, and leans against it.*)

DON. (*Violently, from the hallway.*) I hear you in there! What's this chain doing on the door? Open up, or I'll break the door down!

MARTHA. (*Guiding Deerfield into the garden.*) He'll not only tear you limb from limb, he'll burn every page of your revisions.

DEERFIELD. In that case, I'd better go.

DON. (*From hallway, getting door open a bit again.*) What's going on in there?

DEERFIELD. Good-bye, Juliet. Good-bye, Martha. Tell Polly I'm sorry about this afternoon, but tomorrow's another day.

MARTHA. This kid never gives up. (*Deefield tosses his coat and briefcase to the top of the wall. He tries to climb up a trellis, it breaks. He uses a tree for a ladder, attains the top of the wall.*)

DON. (*From hallway.*) So help me, I'll break the door down! (*Deerfield vanishes over the wall. Martha hurries down* C. *steps to couch.*)

MARTHA. (*To Juliet.*) Okay, let the drawbridge down. (*Juliet removes the chain, and comes down* C. *steps to* D. R. C. *Don, who has evidently drawn back, in hallway, to smash at the door with his shoulder, comes racing down the C. steps and into the room. Martha barely gets out of his way.)*

DON. *(Furious, to Juliet.)* What kind of a way is that to open a door?

JULIET. What kind of a way is that to come into a room?

DON. Never mind! Where are they?

MARTHA. *(Indicating garden.)* One of the love birds just flew the coop. *(Don dashes up C. steps and into the garden. The phone on ledge rings and Juliet goes to it.)*

DON. He broke my trellis and smashed my petunias!

JULIET. *(Answering phone.)* Hello and you sure picked a fine time to call. *(Looking into garden.)* No, Deerfield just stepped out. . . . Yes, I'm sure Mrs. Emerson will be in this evening. I'll give her the message. *(She hangs up.)*

DON. *(Angrily, coming to above C. of the railing.)* You let him escape!

MARTHA. We fought like tigers.

JULIET. But he got away from us.

DON. *(Crossing to bedroom door.)* He didn't get away from Polly! *(Caustically.)* Where is the innocent little girl from Akron who married me to learn all about life? *(Flings open bedroom door.)*

GLORIA. *(Startled, o. s., in bedroom.)* Hey!

DON. Sorry, I keep forgetting Don doesn't live here any more.

JULIET. *(As Don slams bedroom door shut.)* Mr. Emerson, there's no need to be upset. Things like this happen ever day.

DON. Not to me, they don't. *(Angrily, going to Juliet at C.)* And where were you? I told you never to leave them alone.

JULIET. *(With a jumping gesture toward the garden wall.)* Who knew he was a jackrabbit?

DON. You're fired!

JULIET. You can't fire me.

DON. Why can't I?

JULIET. I know too much. *(Don, in exasperation, turns on Martha, who speaks before he can open his mouth.)*

MARTHA. Me, neither. I know where the bodies were buried. *(Self-consciously brushes a crumb from couch.)*

DON. *(Sitting on R. arm of couch.)* How could she do this to

57

me? In the morning at that? (*Martha motions Juliet to go about her work. Juliet shrugs, goes into bedroom, closes door.*)

MARTHA. (*Honestly.*) Polly's a woman, Don. And it's hard to predict what a woman will or won't do when a man is after her. I know I had a lot of affairs that I could never explain to myself later. I used to blame it on nervousness.

DON. That was years ago.

MARTHA. The memory lingers on.

DON. Times have changed.

MARTHA. Women haven't.

DON. But Polly! Only this morning she was talking about a lunch-hour rendezvous at the Waldorf.

MARTHA. With you?

DON. Of course with me! Did you really see anything, Martha? Are you sure? You didn't imagine the whole thing through an alcoholic haze?

MARTHA. I saw what I saw. I'm sorry, Don.

DON. Where did it happen?

MARTHA. Move a foot to the left and you're Deerfield. (*Don jumps off the couch as if he's been stabbed. He looks at the spot in horror.*)

DON. Right there?

MARTHA. It'll look like a new couch if you put on slip covers.

DON. (*Goes to chair, R., sits, wearily.*) Do you know the worst part of the whole thing?

MARTHA. Gee, I hope so.

DON. He not only played around with Polly, he can write.

MARTHA. When did you read his show? You said you'd never look at a line of it.

DON. I read it secretly. By flashlight under the electric blanket.

MARTHA. (*Rises. A step toward Don, speaking gently.*) How about a drink?

DON. No, thanks.

MARTHA. (*Crossing up C. steps to bar—mixes a drink.*) It'll sober you up.

DON. Funny how a man never really knows the woman he's married to.

MARTHA. Funny how a man never really knows the man he is or isn't.

DON. (*Watching her as she moves above him and comes down C.

steps to his R.) Please, I can't take philosophy without a glass of tea.

MARTHA. (*Offering him her drink.*) Have a little Lipton's. One hundred proof. (*Don declines.*) This isn't philosophy, Don. This is common sense. I'll bet you haven't the remotest idea why Polly decided to dilly-dally with the kid from Connecticut.

DON. I'm not interested.

MARTHA. (D. R. *of Don.*) No, all you've been interested in is the competition between you and Polly. Will she become a star before you become a famous playwright? Or vice versa. Neither one of you is willing to settle for the talents you do have. Polly for being a wonderful wife and the mother of your children—and you for writing the best ad copy in town. Why don't you two call it a draw? (*Sits, fireplace bench.*)

DON. How do we do that?

MARTHA. Easy. Stop writing plays and concentrate on making Polly happy instead of ambitious.

DON. You don't think very much of my plays, do you?

MARTHA. Tell me somebody who does.

DON. All right, I will. My new one's going on.

MARTHA. That's hard to believe. I read it.

DON. So did a little group down in the Village. The Octagon Theatre. They think I'm the perfect octagonal writer.

MARTHA. But they don't even use scenery.

DON. (*Going to cabinet* U. C. *behind couch, gets pile of scripts, tied together with cord.*) They say it's much better that way. (*Starting for bedroom with scripts.*) Hang around until I pack and I'll drop you off.

MARTHA. (*Rising, goes to* L. *of Don.*) Pack? Where are you going?

DON. To find an apartment in the Village. I want to be near my play.

MARTHA. What about Polly?

DON. What about her?

MARTHA. Do you want some advice from a battle-scarred veteran?

DON. No. (*Goes to bedroom door, stops without turning.*) What were you going to say?

MARTHA. Forgive her.

DON. Not a chance!

MARTHA. They do parole first offenders.

DON. How do we know today was the first time? No. If she can do this to me—and on the very furniture her mother gave us ——

MARTHA. You can sell the furniture!

DON. What do you expect me to do? Pretend it never happened?

MARTHA. Yes, if you love her.

DON. (*Turning, vehemently.*) Of course I love the double-crossing little two-timer! That's why I'm so damn mad!

MARTHA. I'm so damn glad to hear you say it.

DON. I'm not!

MARTHA. Now that you've forgiven her ——

DON. Who's forgiven her? Just because I'm crazy about her? No, sir, not me! I'm one husband who won't forgive and forget. I don't care how miserable I'm going to be without her!

MARTHA. Okay, Don. Happy Octagon Theatre. (*Don opens bedroom door. Gloria emerges, wearing a sexy hostess gown.*)

GLORIA. (*Crossing toward Martha.*) Don't you ever knock?

DON. I'm sorry, Madame Pompadour. (*He exits into bedroom.*)

GLORIA. What's he in such a tizzy about?

MARTHA. He's got reasons. They're trying out his new play and a new playwright is trying out his old wife.

GLORIA. (*Crossing through C.*) It's been quite a morning around here. I need some hot coffee. How about you, Martha?

MARTHA. Just a jigger. No soda. (*Gloria exits into kitchen. Juliet backs out of bedroom door, carrying an armful of dirty linen.*)

JULIET. (*Calling off, into bedroom.*) That's no way to talk to me, Mr. Emerson. If you can't keep your wife contented, that's your problem, not mine. I had an uncle once who —— (*The bedroom door is slammed in her face. She turns to Martha.*) That's exactly what Uncle Maxwell did to my aunt. Slammed the door on her. There was one difference, of course. Her head was in it at the time. (*Don opens bedroom door, angrily.*)

DON. Where the hell are my clean shirts?

JULIET. Getting cleaned!

MARTHA. You'll only need T-shirts in the Village. (*There is a loud knock at the front door.*)

DON. Who the hell is that?

JULIET. (*Going to door.*) How do I know? Mr. Emerson, you've blown your top. You've goofed. (*Juliet goes up C. steps and opens*

*the door. Two uniformed Policemen push Deerfield onto the land-
ing. Deerfield's tie is askew, and the First Policeman carries the
briefcase.)*

FIRST POLICEMAN. *(Turning to Don, as Juliet clears back in
fright.)* You Donald W. Emerson?

DON. *(Moving toward C. steps.)* That's right.

FIRST POLICEMAN. *(Indicating Deerfield.)* You know this man?

DEERFIELD. Of course he does.

FIRST POLICEMAN. Shut up. We caught him climbing over the
garden wall with this briefcase. Got your name on it. *(Hands
briefcase to Don.)*

DON. *(Taking briefcase.)* It's mine, all right. *(Puts case on
phonograph cabinet.)*

SECOND POLICEMAN. He put up some fight when we started
to bring him back here.

FIRST POLICEMAN. He bit me.

DEERFIELD. It was an accident.

FIRST POLICEMAN. Accident! *(Pulls blood-soaked, bandaged
thumb from pocket.)* My thumb is hangin' by the roots! *(To
Don.)* Claims he's a friend of yours.

DON. Friend! Oh, he's much more than a friend.

DEERFIELD. *(To Policemen.)* See? It's all a mistake. It only
happened because I left in a hurry.

FIRST POLICEMAN. Over that wall?

MARTHA. We never could train him to use doors.

DEERFIELD. Tell them who I am, Mr. Emerson. I have a lot of
work to do.

DON. You've done a day's work, you four-eyed home-breaker!
*(He rushes up R. steps to take a punch at Deerfield. The Second
Policeman tries to protect Deerfield, and gets the punch in the
face. He falls on the platform, L. The First Policeman pushes Don
back down the R. steps.)*

FIRST POLICEMAN. Who do you think you are, hitting an
officer? *(He pulls Deerfield, who has moved forward on platform,
back into custody.)*

DON. Who does he think he is, trying to keep me from punching
him? *(He comes back on R. steps and tries to swing at Deerfield
again, but this time the First Policeman gets in the way, and goes
down with the blow.)*

61

FIRST POLICEMAN. (*On his knees, above the planter* R.) Hey, you bloodied my nose!

DON. I still haven't hit the right guy! (*The Second Policeman starts for Don, and is given a punch that sends him sprawling down the* C. *steps, over the back of the First Policeman. Deerfield starts for the front door, but Don struggles with Deerfield just above the umbrella stand. The First Policeman grabs Don's ankle. The Second Policeman holds onto the foot of the First Policeman. The group freezes as Gloria emerges from the kitchen with a cup of coffee.*)

MARTHA. (*Studying the tableau by the door.*) I swear I saw that at the Metropolitan Museum. (*The Policemen get to their feet, and pull Don and Deerfield apart. First Policeman brings Don* D. C. *on platform at top of steps.*)

SECOND POLICEMAN. (*Clutching Deerfield, speaks to Don.*) All right, buddy, you asked for it. We're going to prefer charges against you.

DON. Prefer them! I'm going down to the station and prefer charges against *him!* Impairing the morals of an adult!

DEERFIELD. Why are you so mad at me? All I did was to take your briefcase.

DON. Just don't put me in the same car with him!

GLORIA. (*Bewildered.*) I wish somebody would tell me what happened.

DON. (*A step along platform toward her, dragging the First Policeman with him.*) I'll tell you what's going to happen. You're going to pack up and leave! I know who advised Polly to do what she did. You've slept in my bed for the last time!

FIRST POLICEMAN. Who's Polly?

DON. My wife, and keep your bloody nose out of this!

SECOND POLICEMAN. (*To Deerfield.*) Let's go, buster.

DEERFIELD. Martha, you can explain everything.

DON. (*Grimly.*) She did. Let's go, buster. (*First Policeman pulls Don* L. *on platform, picks up briefcase from top of phonograph cabinet, hands it to Martha.*)

FIRST POLICEMAN. Here you are, lady. Mr. Emerson's property.

DEERFIELD. (*Frantically, pushing his head forward under the First Policeman's arm.*) My revisions! The new Civil War!

FIRST POLICEMAN. (*Pushing Deerfield's head back.*) You got

your own right here! (*To Don.*) Come on, Bud. (*Second Police-man takes Deerfield out, First Policeman pulls Don to door. Don catches hold of the moulding.*)

DON. If the office calls, tell them I was unavoidably detained! (*Policeman pulls him out.*)

MARTHA. Oh, the natives were restless tonight!

GLORIA. How did the policemen get into the act?

MARTHA. They were probably taking a smoke in the alley.

JULIET. (*Above railing, proudly.*) Quite a guy, Mr. Emerson. He didn't hit just one cop. He hit two.

MARTHA. The Judge will certainly be amused when he hears that. (*Polly enters the open front door. She closes door, dejectedly.*) Hi! You missed all the excitement.

POLLY. Wasn't that Don and Deerfield I just saw riding away in a police car?

MARTHA. They're going to be character witnesses for each other. (*Gloria has settled on the couch.*)

POLLY. What happened to me today was the worst experience of my life.

MARTHA. All of us are conscience-stricken afterwards. (*Polly tosses her hat and gloves dispiritedly to Juliet, who catches them. Then Polly looks around at her three friends before she speaks.*)

POLLY. (*The tragedienne.*) You don't understand. I'm out of the show. I'm not going to play "Melinda."

MARTHA. After the price you paid this morning?

POLLY. (*Dramatically, moving down L. steps to L. of couch.*) All my life I've worked and slaved for this chance. And then Don did this to me! I thought we had an agreement. I'll never forgive him as long as I live! Never, never, never!

MARTHA. I can't understand why the Actors' Studio turned you down. (*Polly dials at the phone on ledge.*) Why are you out of the show? (*When she doesn't answer.*) Polly, why are you out of the show?

POLLY. Why? I'm going to have a baby! (*Martha goes to railing, c., and shakes hands with Juliet.*)

MARTHA. We did it!

POLLY. Hello—long distance? I want to talk to my mother in Akron——

CURTAIN

63

The same. That evening. The electric blanket is folded neatly on the railing R. *Don's briefcase is on dining table as is Deerfield's.*
Martha backs out of the bedroom, on tiptoe, closing the door, just as Juliet, carrying a large purse, enters from the kitchen. They meet, C.

JULIET. How does she feel?
MARTHA. Pregnant. She insists she felt the baby kick her.
JULIET. That's impossible.
MARTHA. He might be a progressive child. How much money have you got?
JULIET. I've got twenty-five here in my purse. How about you?
MARTHA. (*Opening purse.*) Here's $15. My rent money. (*Removes shoe.*) And I've got another twenty stashed away for a night cap. (*Tries the other shoe.*) Wrong shoe. That's for cab fare in case I get stuck and have to go home alone. (*Takes out $20, folded neatly in shoe.*) This was going to buy a lot of dreams over the rocks.
JULIET. How much do we need to bail out Mr. Emerson?
MARTHA. When I talked to him on the phone, he said a hundred dollars and not to bother. He wants to stay in jail for the rest of his life. (*Juliet finds some bills in her purse, then puts the purse on the* C. *hassock.*)
JULIET. With my twenty-five, that makes sixty. What are you going to tell Mr. Emerson after you bail him out?
MARTHA. Nothing. Absolutely nothing. I wouldn't deny Polly the pleasure of showing Don what a fool he made of himself. Thanks to me, of course. We're still forty dollars short.
JULIET. I haven't gone into my savings accounts yet. (*Reaching into one stocking.*) Here's ten more. (*Reaching into other stocking.*) And ten more. (*Reaching into bosom.*) And twenty more makes it an even hundred. (*Deposits bills in Martha's hat, which Martha holds, inverted, for the purpose.*)

MARTHA. What kind of a way is that to carry money?

JULIET. You never know which pocket is going to be picked. (*Picks up purse again.*)

MARTHA. (*As they both move up* C. *steps to front door.*) Poor Don. This whole thing happened because I was so woozy. I was sure it was Polly on the couch with Deerfield. I even heard him say, "Polly, my sweet—Polly, my darling."

JULIET. Liquor is a terrible thing.

MARTHA. Oh, you're so right. I'm going to give it up, Juliet. I've learned my lesson. (*Opens door.*)

JULIET. You mean you're going on the wagon?

MARTHA. May the ceiling fall down on me if I ever touch another drop. (*She exits. There is a sharp crash* O. S. *in hallway. Martha returns, carrying a chunk of plaster, which she hands to Juliet.*) This place is falling apart. (*Exits. Juliet tosses the chunk of plaster into a plant near the front door. The bedroom door opens, and Polly appears, wearing an attractive negligee and carrying a tiny lace handkerchief to sniffle into.*)

POLLY. Don! Is that you, Don? (*Moves across to couch.*)

JULIET. (*Crossing around to* D. L.) No, it was Martha. She went to bail out the father of your child. I thought you never wanted to see him again.

POLLY. I—I don't. Not ever. He was horrible—to think I'd be unfaithful to him—and on Mamma's couch.

JULIET. Is Gloria packed yet?

POLLY. She's taking a shower.

JULIET. (*With a look around.*) That's all she's taking. I checked everything. (*The front doorbell rings.*)

POLLY. If it's anybody, I don't want to see them. Not in my condition. (*Exits into bedroom.*)

JULIET. (*Going to front door.*) It hardly shows. (*Juliet opens the door. Granville Prescott, a man in his fifties, who looks as impressive as his money, steps in briskly.*)

PRESCOTT. How do you do?

JULIET. (*Closing door.*) How do you do?

PRESCOTT. I'm sorry to be so late. Does Mrs. Emerson plan to go somewhere for the evening?

JULIET. Mrs. Emerson doesn't plan to go anywhere for nine months.

PRESCOTT. (*Handing Juliet his hat, coat and scarf which she puts on bench by front door.*) Splendid! I want to have a long talk with her. You did give her my message?

JULIET. Oh, was that you who called before?

PRESCOTT. (*Coming down C. steps. Crossing down to R. bassock.*) Would you be kind enough to tell her that Mr. Prescott is here? Mr. Granville Prescott.

JULIET. (*Coming down steps to L. of Prescott.*) Prescott, like in Deerfield?

PRESCOTT. Oh, you know my son?

JULIET. Considering he's been just as good as living here, yes.

PRESCOTT. That's exactly what I wish to discuss with Mrs. Emerson. (*Confidentially.*) Tell me, what does she see in the boy?

JULIET. I'll call her. I got dishes to finish up. (*As Juliet goes to bedroom door, Prescott moves C. Juliet raps on door.*) Gentleman in the parlor! (*She puts her hand on her hip and ogles Prescott, who is amused.*)

GLORIA. (*From bedroom.*) I'll be right out.

JULIET. Not you. Mrs. Emerson. (*As Juliet starts through C., Prescott crosses below her to the R. chair, sits.*) I like the way you sat down.

PRESCOTT. (*Astonished.*) Thank you. I always sit down this way.

JULIET. I say a man's bottom is the index to his character.

PRESCOTT. Thank you.

JULIET. You've got a lot of character, Mr. Prescott. (*Moving to kitchen door.*) And a very good index. (*Exits to kitchen.*)

PRESCOTT. (*Looking after her.*) Thank you. Thank you very much. (*Polly enters from bedroom, to D. R. Prescott rises.*)

POLLY. You wanted to see me?

PRESCOTT. Yes. Yes, I did. Deerfield wrote his mother how he felt about you.

POLLY. You're his father?

PRESCOTT. So I've been led to believe. Over the years I've fallen into the habit of reading Mrs. Prescott's mail. That's how I found out what's been going on.

POLLY. Mr. Prescott, I don't know what Deerfield wrote his mother, but nothing's been going on. He's never even kissed me.

PRESCOTT. You don't have to protect him, my dear. I'm a man of the world.

POLLY. I'm not protecting him. He's always been a perfect gentleman.

PRESCOTT. You're only saying that to make me feel bad.

POLLY. (*Sitting, fireplace bench.*) No, I'm not, Mr. Prescott. It's true.

PRESCOTT. (*Moves* c.) It's disgraceful! Why, when I was his age my father had to buy off four women, including one who split the money with me. (*Sits* R. *hassock, distressed.*) This is most disillusioning. His mother and I had high hopes that the boy was having an affair with you. (*Unconvinced.*) Are you sure he isn't?

POLLY. I couldn't be surer. (*Rises, crosses to him.*) I found out today that I'm going to have a baby.

PRESCOTT. You are? (*Elated.*) Why, that's wonderful! I couldn't be more delighted. (*Rises.*) May I use your phone to tell his mother?

POLLY. Certainly. It's right over there.

PRESCOTT. (*Crossing to phone on ledge.*) Thank you.

POLLY. His mother? Why would she be interested?

PRESCOTT. (*Dialing.*) I don't blame you for denying everything, but now that Granville Prescott the Second is on his way, you don't have to cover up any more. (*Into phone.*) Westport 7612 and reverse the charges. (*To Polly.*) No love child will ever have more doting grandparents.

POLLY. (*Crossing to* R. *of Prescott.*) Mr. Prescott, he's not a love child, and you're not his grandparents.

PRESCOTT. I'll call my lawyer and set up a trust fund for the boy.

POLLY. I don't think Don will take the money. He's very strange about things like that.

PRESCOTT. Who's Don?

POLLY. My husband. I loathe and despise him right now, but he's the only one who could be the baby's father.

PRESCOTT. (*Suspiciously.*) How do you know?

POLLY. (*Crossing to* R. *of couch.*) I know. The way I feel about him, I wish it were somebody else's. I wish I could name ten men as its father!

PRESCOTT. (*Crosses to back of* L. *end of couch, with phone.*) Would one of them be my son?

POLLY. (*Sits, couch.*) He'd be at the bottom of the list.

PRESCOTT. (*Sits back of couch, L. end.*) This is terrible. What am I going to tell his poor mother?

POLLY. Tell her the truth.

PRESCOTT. She's not used to that from me. (*Into phone.*) Hello, Margaret. I have bad news. Very bad news. It isn't true—not any of it. (*Listens for a moment.*) Nothing's happened between them. The boy's no good, I tell you. He belongs in the factory where a good strong girl on the assembly line can take him apart. (*Listens.*) Hold on, I'll try to find out. (*To Polly.*) Do you know where Deerfield is now?

POLLY. In jail.

PRESCOTT. In jail? (*A take, delighted.*) In jail!

POLLY. For hitting a policeman.

PRESCOTT. (*Rising, speaks happily into phone.*) Margaret, everything's going to be all right! Our boy's in jail! (*He laughs, delightedly.*) Call you back later! (*Hangs up.*)

POLLY. Mr. Prescott, he didn't really hit him. He bit him.

PRESCOTT. What's the difference? He made physical contact, didn't he? (*Crossing through C. up steps to get hat and coat and scarf from bench by front door.*) I must go bail out the tiger. This ought to make a great change in him—having a prison record. Don't you think so, young lady?

POLLY. (*Crossing to below R. of C. steps.*) I'm not a young lady any more. I'm a matron now. And Don did it deliberately, I'm sure.

PRESCOTT. (*Crossing down C. steps to L. of Polly.*) Did what?

POLLY. Made me a mother so I couldn't be a star. A girl has a right to know when she's going to have a baby. Don took advantage of my good nature.

PRESCOTT. (*Taking her hand, kisses it.*) And you appeal to mine, Mrs. Emerson. Don't you worry. I'll find a way for you to have the baby and the part of Melinda. (*Front door opens, and Don enters with Martha. Prescott breaks L. C.*)

DON. Sorry, I should have knocked.

POLLY. Oh, it's you. What are you doing here?

DON. I live here. I've got squatter's rights on that couch.

MARTHA. (*Closing door.*) This is Don, Polly. Remember? (*To Prescott.*) He's been away, doing time. (*Goes to bar, fixes drink.*)

DON. Never mind who I am. (*Indicating Prescott.*) Who's he?

POLLY. Deerfield's father.

DON. I always thought he was just a legend.

POLLY. Mr. Prescott, I want you to meet the man who ruined my life.

PRESCOTT. How do you do?

DON. (*To Polly—coming down* C. *steps.*) I ruined your life? What about mine? What about what happened this morning?

POLLY. (*To Martha.*) Martha, didn't you tell him?

MARTHA. Not the late late news. I wanted you to tell him yourself.

DON. Yes, you tell me, my sweet. How are you going to explain everything—even though it won't do any good?

POLLY. I'm not even going to bother.

DON. Oh, just throw yourself on the mercy of the court.

POLLY. I wish somebody would tell me why I married you.

DON. If I think of an answer, I'll drop you a post card.

POLLY. Not at this address. I'll be in Akron.

DON. Oh, no you won't. You're staying right here. I'm not going to be stuck with the custody of that maid your mother palmed off on us. I'll be packed and out of your way in no time.

POLLY. You going home to *your* mother?

DON. (*Crossing up* C. *steps to landing.*) I'm going back to the only life fit for a man. Bachelorhood. Carousing when he feels like it. Staying up as late as he pleases. Going out with all the girls who'll go out with him. Any man who gives that up must be crazy.

PRESCOTT and MARTHA. (*Simultaneously.*) Insane.

DON. (*Crossing through* C. *steps to* D. L. *of coffee table.*) Would I be imposing if I had a last cup of coffee before I left?

POLLY. I suppose you want me to get it for you?

DON. No, thanks. You never could make a good cup of coffee. To say nothing of the fact that your eggs-over-easy were always too loose or too hard. And what you did with a good steak!

POLLY. Donald Waldo Emerson—I loathe and despise you!

DON. I don't feel that way about you. I just have pity for you. To think you'd carry on with someone like Deerfield. (*To Prescott.*) Begging your pardon.

PRESCOTT. Oh, that's all right. I feel the same way about him.

DON. Don't let your son get involved with her any further, Mr. Prescott. She's older than she looks.

PRESCOTT. (*A step toward Don, below couch.*) Young man,

speaking from experience, I'd say you are madly in love with your beautiful wife.

DON. Beautiful? Have you ever seen her in the morning without make-up?

PRESCOTT. I haven't been that fortunate.

DON. (*Making bleary-eyed face, pulling down lower lids.*) It's frightening! (*Exits, kitchen.*)

POLLY. What's the penalty for justifiable homicide in this state?

MARTHA. (*Comes to head of* C. *steps with glass.*) Anybody else want one of these? Scotch over Scotch.

PRESCOTT. Mrs. Emerson, I'm a bit confused. You didn't have a liaison with my son, but he thinks you did?

POLLY. You heard him.

PRESCOTT. You're going to have a baby, but he doesn't know?

MARTHA. (*Crossing through* C. *to kitchen door* D. L.—*along platform—comes down* L. *steps.*) We run more puzzle contests than the *Daily News*. After all the lies I've told him, I don't know if he'll believe the truth. (*Starts to take a drink, looks at ceiling apprehensively, exits into kitchen.*)

PRESCOTT. (*Goes to Polly.*) I like your husband, Mrs. Emerson. He knows how to insult a woman and not mean a word of it. Now, where were we?

POLLY. I was going to play the part of "Melinda" and have the baby, too.

PRESCOTT. And so you shall. I promise you. Shall we seal the bargain with a kiss—on the cheek?

POLLY. I don't see anything wrong with it at your age. (*Prescott winces, and she holds up her face. As he leans forward, there is a crash from the garden. This proves only a temporary distraction to Prescott, who completes the kiss. Just then Deerfield bounds into the garden. He is aghast at what he sees.*)

DEERFIELD. Dad! (*Rushes forward, vaulting over platform railing.*)

PRESCOTT. (*Flustered, turning to Deerfield at* C.) Is that how your mother and I taught you to enter a room?

DEERFIELD. Polly, he's old enough to be my father!

PRESCOTT. Please remember I am. You're supposed to be in jail, young man.

DEERFIELD. Mr. Emerson didn't prefer charges, so they let me go.

POLLY. I'm glad.

70

DEERFIELD. I came back for my briefcase. The new Deerfield needs it.

POLLY. The new Deerfield?

DEERFIELD. (*Crosses to bottom c. step, between them.*) I'm a different man since this afternoon. I'm not the same fellow. Can't you tell?

POLLY. You look exactly the same to me.

DEERFIELD. No, I'm different. I've got guts now. I didn't know I had any till I stood up to those policemen. Now I'm even going to fight the rebels from Atlanta. (*Goes up c. steps to dining table on platform, and begins transferring papers from Don's briefcase to his own.*)

PRESCOTT. (*Puzzled, following Deerfield to R. of table.*) The who from where?

DEERFIELD. The backers of my show.

PRESCOTT. What are they doing to you, my boy?

DEERFIELD. They can take their Confederate money and secede again!

POLLY. (*Moves up c. steps to R. of Prescott.*) But "Melinda" has to go on. It's a beautiful show.

PRESCOTT. (*Turns to Polly, smiling.*) Of course it has to go on. I'll put up the money myself and charge it to institutional advertising.

DEERFIELD. (*Suspiciously.*) Under what conditions? (*To Polly.*) He always has conditions.

PRESCOTT. If you'll wait a year.

DEERFIELD. A year? Why should I wait a year?

PRESCOTT. So Polly can play Melinda. She's going to have a baby.

DEERFIELD. (*Coming between them, astonished.*) A baby?

PRESCOTT. Of course one of the conditions is that you work in the factory for the year.

POLLY. (*Hopefully.*) Would you? I'm sure the Civil War won't get dated.

PRESCOTT. You always told me your music was ahead of its time. This would help close the gap.

POLLY. The baby won't be in the way at rehearsals.

DEERFIELD. (*Stubbornly.*) I said I wouldn't take a cent for the show from my father.

71

PRESCOTT. It's all government money. They'd want you to have it.

DEERFIELD. No dream sequences, and the North wins tne Civil War. Okay, I'll do it!

POLLY. (*Elated.*) I'm back in the show!

PRESCOTT. Just like I promised. Why don't we all go out and celebrate?

POLLY. That's a wonderful idea! (*Crosses down R. steps to bedroom door.*) It won't take me a minute to get dressed.

PRESCOTT. What about Don?

POLLY. (*Airily.*) Who's he? (*The front doorbell rings.*) See who it is, would you? (*She exits into bedroom. Deerfield opens the front door, revealing Penelope. She is obviously Vassar, wears heavy shell-rim glasses, and carries a folded newspaper.*)

DEERFIELD. Penelope!

PENELOPE. (*Entering.*) Deerfield! You've escaped!

DEERFIELD. What are you doing here?

PENELOPE. It's in all the papers about you. (*Reads headlines.*) "Playboy Playwright Slugs Cop."

PRESCOTT. May I see the newspaper, young lady?

PENELOPE. Of course. (*She hands it to him without taking her adoring eyes off Deerfield.*)

PRESCOTT. (*Reads headline.*) "Playboy Playwright Slugs Cop." "See story on page five." (*Turns pages, glowering.*) What's the story doing way back there?

PENELOPE. I was never so thrilled in my life.

DEERFIELD. All I did was bite him.

PRESCOTT. (*Elated.*) Thank heavens we have a free press in this country! They've distorted the story beautifully. (*Crosses between them, picking up coat, scarf and hat from bench.*) Young man, would you tell Mrs. Emerson that I went down to the corner for the other papers? I'll wait for her in the car.

DEERFIELD. Yes, sir. Good night, sir.

PRESCOTT. (*Shakes Deerfield's hand.*) Good night, son. Keep punching in there! (*Exits, laughing, closing door.*)

PENELOPE. (*Puzzled.*) Who is he?

DEERFIELD. Oh, I found him here kissing Mrs. Emerson.

PENELOPE. First her husband, then you, and now she's carrying on with that old man?

DEERFIELD. I don't think it's anything serious. It was sort of a fatherly kiss.

PENELOPE. I'd settle for any kind. In all my life I've never been kissed by a man who bit a policeman. (*Moves closer.*)

DEERFIELD. I don't know why I want to kiss you, Penelope, but suddenly I do. It must be the new Deerfield.

PENELOPE. What's the difference from the old one?

DEERFIELD. (*Leads her down* C. *steps.*) The new one doesn't talk about things. He does them—with technique and finesse. (*Takes her to the couch.*) Let's go over to my work bench. (*Sits, pulls Penelope down beside him.*) See the difference?

PENELOPE. (*Happily.*) It's different, all right. The last time we ——

DEERFIELD. You talk too much. (*Holds her face up to his.*) Do you have to keep your glasses on?

PENELOPE. No. Do you?

DEERFIELD. No. (*They both turn front, remove glasses in unison, feel for a place on coffee table to put glasses down, then, bent over coffee table, both look into one another's eyes—at very close range.*) Why, Penelope, you're beautiful!

PENELOPE. (*Breathlessly.*) You're handsome!

DEERFIELD. Can you really see what I look like with your glasses off?

PENELOPE. No.

DEERFIELD. Me, neither.

PENELOPE. It doesn't matter. We can grope our way to love!

DEERFIELD. Penelope, I feel like we're the last two people on earth! (*They go into a passionate embrace as Don and Martha enter from kitchen.*)

DON. They're at it again!

MARTHA. Same boy, new girl. (*Deerfield and Penelope break, and look at each other.*)

DEERFIELD. Why didn't you tell me you were like this?

PENELOPE. All Vassar girls are pent-up.

DEERFIELD. What would you like for breakfast?

PENELOPE. (*As they both sit up.*) Breakfast?

DEERFIELD. We can pick up a week's supply on the way to my apartment. (*Don clears his throat. Penelope looks startled.*)

PENELOPE. Deerfield, there's someone here!

DEERFIELD. That's impossible. We're the last two people on earth. (*They put their glasses on.*)

DON. No, there are four of us now. You must be Penelope, judging by your uniform. I'm delighted to see you take advantage of my ex-cellmate.

PENELOPE. (*Who has risen, moves quickly to* C. *on Don's speech.*) It's not like you think at all. I was just —

MARTHA. Doesn't mean a thing. He's always getting caught on that couch.

DEERFIELD. (*To Don.*) You wouldn't sell it to me, would you?

DON. It's a deal! If I can throw in Gloria.

PENELOPE. (*To Deerfield, who does a take.*) Who's Gloria?

DON. Don't ask questions, young lady. Just be satisfied he's yours.

PENELOPE. Why, he's nice, Deerfield. You told me he was horrible.

DON. Oh, I am, I am! I refused to share my wife with him. (*Martha pulls* D. L. *chair from wall, sits.*) I don't believe you've met Martha. She always goes bail for me.

PENELOPE. How do you do?

MARTHA. Oh, I have my moments.

DON. (*To Penelope.*) Did I hear Deerfield invite you over for breakfast?

DEERFIELD. It was a figure of speech. I'll buy her dinner first.

DON. (*To Penelope.*) How can you resist such generosity?

PENELOPE. I can't. To me he's the most attractive man in the world. Even with my glasses on.

MARTHA. Who's your oculist?

DON. (*To Deerfield, as he crosses up* L. *steps and opens front door.*) Get the right briefcase—and you have my permission to use the door when you leave this time.

DEERFIELD. (*Crossing up* L. *steps to dining table, with Penelope.*) Will you explain everything to Polly?

DON. I'll try, if she ever talks to me again after the way I behaved. Martha, how could you make such a mistake?

MARTHA. How could you believe me?

PENELOPE. (*Her arms around Deerfield.*) I can't believe that he's mine, finally. All mine!

DEERFIELD. (*Caught in her squeeze.*) Only because I'm the new —Deer—field ——

PENELOPE. No, only because of Passion Flower.

DON. Passion Flower?

PENELOPE. That's the new perfume advertised in the New Yorker this week.

DON. Good God! I wrote that ad!

PENELOPE. I've got four ounces all over me.

DON. You don't believe that stuff?

PENELOPE. (*Crossing between Deerfield and Don.*) Why shouldn't I? Like you said, "It sweeps a man off his feet and into the arms of the woman who wants him." You're a fine writer, Mr. Emerson.

DON. (*Bows to Penelope.*) Thanks. I'll be by to pick up my Pulitzer Prize.

PENELOPE. (*Pulling Deerfield out the front door.*) Shall we go, darling? I'm starved.

DEERFIELD. (*Sniffing her perfume.*) I'm working up quite an appetite myself. (*He waves good-bye, exits with Penelope. Door remains open. Polly enters from bedroom, wearing a trim little suit and carrying her hat and purse.*)

POLLY. Where's Mr. Prescott?

DON. Mr. Prescott just left to attend the first annual Yale-Vassar game.

POLLY. And why haven't you left yet? You've had your coffee.

DON. I've got a date with a girl from Akron.

POLLY. Anyone I know?

DON. She might be. Especially since I found out it wasn't you on the couch with Deerfield.

POLLY. What else did you find out?

DON. I found out I wasn't really jealous of you and Deerfield. I did a lot of thinking while I was in the kitchen.

POLLY. I'll read the book when it comes out.

DON. No, I want you to hear this now. It was only his damn talent and my lack of it. I couldn't put my name on the ads I wrote, but I wanted it on something.

POLLY. Well, it will be. The baby might even look like you.

DON. What baby?

POLLY. (*To Martha who has moved up a couple of the L. steps.*) Why didn't you tell him about *that*?

MARTHA. It's customary for the wife, not the midwife, to break the news. (*Don continues to look at Polly, as if in a trance.*)

POLLY. Don, what are you staring at?

DON. Who's staring?

MARTHA. Snap your fingers under his nose.

DON. (*Crosses to Polly, speaks to Martha, without turning to her.*) Go away, Martha. Get lost.

MARTHA. That should be easy in a town this size.

DON. Aren't you gone yet? I would like to be alone with the mother of my child. (*Gloria enters from bedroom, ready to depart. She moves to landing, carrying two pieces of luggage.*)

GLORIA. Hi, Martha! I see you got him out of jail. (*Juliet enters from kitchen, wearing coat and the new green hat.*)

JULIET. Oh, hello, Mr. Emerson. How was jail?

DON. The cooking was better.

GLORIA. Juliet, would you be good enough to help me with the rest of my luggage?

JULIET. It'll be a pleasure. (*Exits into bedroom.*)

GLORIA. Before I leave, I want to thank you for everything, Don. I know I crowded you a little.

DON. Forget it. I behaved like a monster.

GLORIA. I needed to be around friends while I thought everything out.

POLLY. Gloria's going back to her second husband. (*Juliet brings Gloria's luggage from bedroom, sets it on landing.*)

MARTHA. (*At railing, L., shocked.*) The one without money? That's crazy!

GLORIA. He was the only one I really loved. A girl just has to follow her heart.

DON. When did you find that out?

GLORIA. When he phoned tonight and told me about finding oil on this little piece of property in Texas. (*Crosses to Polly and embraces her.*) Good-bye, Polly—you'll have a beautiful baby.

POLLY. Stay happy!

MARTHA. Stay rich!

DON. Stay married, for a change.

GLORIA. 'Bye, everyone! (*She goes up C. steps and exits—carrying the two bags.*)

MARTHA. (*Moving to door.*) I might as well follow her to the airport. There's a little bar out there that's virgin territory for me.

JULIET. (*On landing, R. of Martha.*) I'll go with you. It's time I found out how the other half drinks.

MARTHA. What'll we use for money?

76

JULIET. (*Tapping bosom.*) I got resources I haven't even tapped yet! (*Exits with two of Gloria's bags.*)

MARTHA. (*Struggling with the largest of Gloria's bags.*) Take my advice, kids. Lock the door and turn off the phone. You're only young once, even though I'm trying to prove otherwise.

DON. Let me help you.

MARTHA. No, thanks. I work alone. But not for much longer, maybe. In all the excitement, I forgot to tell you—I got a proposal of marriage today.

POLLY. Why, that's wonderful, Martha!

DON. It really is. Who's the lucky man?

MARTHA. Mahoney. Who else? (*Exits with the bag.*)

DON. (*Closing door, turns to Polly.*) Why didn't you tell me you wanted a baby?

POLLY. I didn't know I did. Not until a few minutes ago.

DON. A few minutes ago?

POLLY. It was the way you looked at me—when you found out you were going to be a father.

DON. I always look that way when I'm startled.

POLLY. This was a special look of startlement. Like you were the first man on the moon.

DON. (*Looking at her, but not making a move.*) How do you feel?

POLLY. I feel like I always feel—all right.

DON. What are you going to name the baby?

POLLY. (*Teasing.*) Melinda?

DON. Melinda! What kind of a name is that for a boy?

POLLY. You can call him Mel for short.

DON. (*Goes to Polly.*) Well, the three of us can talk it over, now that we're alone. (*Doorbell rings.*)

POLLY. (*Crossing to up C. steps door.*) Martha must have forgotten her umbrella again. (*She opens the front door and discloses Mrs. Johnson, loaded with luggage.*) My mother!

MRS. JOHNSON. (*Dropping bags, rushes to embrace Polly.*) My baby!

DON. My God! (*As Polly and her mother embrace, Don grabs the electric blanket from the railing and starts to make up his bed on the couch.*)

CURTAIN

LI'L OL' YOU AND LI'L OL' ME

LYRIC BY
LEO ROBIN

MUSIC BY
JULE STYNE

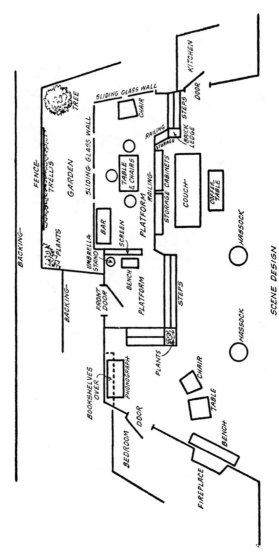

SCENE DESIGN

"*WAKE UP, DARLING*".

PROPERTY PLOT

Act I—Scene 1

On dining table: portable typewriter, paper, carbons, pencils, etc., ashtray

On bench by front door: Martha's hat, gloves and purse. In purse: shoes and earrings

On coffee table: ashtray, lighter, box of cigarettes

Umbrellas in stand by front door

Phone on coffee table, phone on phonograph

In cabinet behind couch: pile of scripts tied with cord

Ashtray on table at R.

Don: briefcase, pipe, cigarettes, lighter, key

Martha: cigarettes

Polly: hat, gloves, purse

Deerfield: eyeglasses, dime, cigarette lighter, notebook and pencil

Offstage for Juliet: 6 cokes in paper carrier, bottle of liquor in paper bag

2 shopping bags of groceries

Off L. for Juliet: place mats, silver, napkins, etc., for setting table

In bar: glasses, bottles of liquor

Off L. for Juliet, freshly starched uniform cap, two unmatched kitchen candles stuck in tops of two wine bottles

On phonograph cabinet: records

Act I—Scene 2

On coffee table basket of fruit, including banana

Strike bottles with candles

Strike dishes, silver, place mats

Put chairs under table

Pick up whiskey glasses, coke bottle and Scotch bottle; put clean glasses on bar

Set large pillow on couch R.

Set electric blanket on couch

Move the small pillow normally on couch to bannister L.

Army rifle off R.

Tray with three coffee cups off L.

5 pieces of luggage off front door

Off R. for Polly: robe, hair ribbon

Gloria: purse with cigarettes in it, mink stole

Martha: hat and purse

Robe off R. for Don

Act II—Scene 1

Typewriter on dining table, paper and carbons in it
Letters on phonograph
Music MS sheets on piano
Strike: rifle, tray with coffee, bowl of fruit, pillows
Open curtains
Set: piano and special chair
2 briefcases on top of piano
Play MS open on dining table
Pencil and eraser near typewriter
Set pillows on ledge
Polly's purse on bench near front door
Deerfield's coat on chair R.
Phone on ledge
Sheets, blanket and pillow on couch
Off L. for Juliet: tray with sandwich and glass of milk, Polly's gloves, small watering can
A second purse for Polly off R.
N. Y. Times off L.
Cup of coffee on tray

Act II—Scene 2

Fresh linen off L. for Juliet
Crumpled linen off R. for Juliet
Pile of scripts tied with cord in cabinet behind couch
Cup of coffee: Gloria
Martha: purse, hat

Act II—Scene 3

Electric blanket folded on railing
Don's briefcases on dining table
Large purse off L. for Juliet, bills in it
Money for Juliet
Martha's purse and hat on bench by front door
Martha: $20 bill in shoe
Large chunk of plaster outside front door
Polly: handkerchief, hat, purse
Penelope: folded newspaper, eyeglasses
Mrs. Johnson: luggage
Strike: typewriter, music from large table, paper from coffee table
Set: 5 pillows on couch
Prescott: hat, coat, scarf
Gloria: Off R., 5 suitcases
Juliet: coat, green hat

NEW PLAYS

★ **AS BEES IN HONEY DROWN by Douglas Carter Beane.** Winner of the John Gassner Playwriting Award. A hot young novelist finds the subject of his new screenplay in a New York socialite who leads him into the world of *Auntie Mame* and *Breakfast at Tiffany's*, before she takes him for a ride. "A delicious soufflé of a satire … [an] extremely entertaining fable for an age that always chooses image over substance." *–The NY Times* "… A witty assessment of one of the most active and relentless industries in a consumer society … the creation of 'hot' young things, which the media have learned to mass produce with efficiency and zeal." *–The NY Daily News* [3M, 3W, flexible casting] ISBN: 0-8222-1651-5

★ **STUPID KIDS by John C. Russell.** In rapid, highly stylized scenes, the story follows four high-school students as they make their way from first through eighth period and beyond, struggling with the fears, frustrations, and longings peculiar to youth. "In STUPID KIDS … playwright John C. Russell gets the opera of adolescence to a T … The stylized teenspeak of STUPID KIDS … suggests that Mr. Russell may have hidden a tape recorder under a desk in study hall somewhere and then scoured the tapes for good quotations … it is the kids' insular, ceaselessly churning world, a pre-adult world of Doritos and libidos, that the playwright seeks to lay bare." *–The NY Times* "STUPID KIDS [is] a sharp-edged … whoosh of teen angst and conformity anguish. It is also very funny." *–NY Newsday* [2M, 2W] ISBN: 0-8222-1698-1

★ **COLLECTED STORIES by Donald Margulies.** From Obie Award-winner Donald Margulies comes a provocative analysis of a student-teacher relationship that turns sour when the protégé becomes a rival. "With his fine ear for detail, Margulies creates an authentic, insular world, and he gives equal weight to the opposing viewpoints of two formidable characters." *–The LA Times* "This is probably Margulies' best play to date …" *–The NY Post* "… always fluid and lively, the play is thick with ideas, like a stock-pot of good stew." *–The Village Voice* [2W] ISBN: 0-8222-1640-X

★ **FREEDOMLAND by Amy Freed.** An overdue showdown between a son and his father sets off fireworks that illuminate the neurosis, rage and anxiety of one family – and of America at the turn of the millennium. "FREEDOMLAND's more obvious links are to *Buried Child* and *Bosoms and Neglect*. Freed, like Guare, is an inspired wordsmith with a gift for surreal touches in situations grounded in familiar and real territory." *–Curtain Up* [3M, 4W] ISBN: 0-8222-1719-8

★ **STOP KISS by Diana Son.** A poignant and funny play about the ways, both sudden and slow, that lives can change irrevocably. "There's so much that is vital and exciting about STOP KISS … you want to embrace this young author and cheer her onto other works … the writing on display here is funny and credible … you also will be charmed by its heartfelt characters and up-to-the-minute humor." *–The NY Daily News* "… irresistibly exciting … a sweet, sad, and enchantingly sincere play." *–The NY Times* [3M, 3W] ISBN: 0-8222-1731-7

★ **THREE DAYS OF RAIN by Richard Greenberg.** The sins of fathers and mothers make for a bittersweet elegy in this poignant and revealing drama. "… a work so perfectly judged it heralds the arrival of a major playwright … Greenberg is extraordinary." *–The NY Daily News* "Greenberg's play is filled with graceful passages that are by turns melancholy, harrowing, and often, quite funny." *–Variety* [2M, 1W] ISBN: 0-8222-1676-0

★ **THE WEIR by Conor McPherson.** In a bar in rural Ireland, the local men swap spooky stories in an attempt to impress a young woman from Dublin who recently moved into a nearby "haunted" house. However, the tables are soon turned when she spins a yarn of her own. "You shed all sense of time at this beautiful and devious new play." *–The NY Times* "Sheer theatrical magic. I have rarely been so convinced that I have just seen a modern classic. Tremendous." *–The London Daily Telegraph* [4M, 1W] ISBN: 0-8222-1706-6

DRAMATISTS PLAY SERVICE, INC.
440 Park Avenue South, New York, NY 10016 212-683-8960 Fax 212-213-1539
postmaster@dramatists.com   www.dramatists.com

NEW PLAYS

★ **CLOSER by Patrick Marber.** Winner of the 1998 Olivier Award for Best Play and the 1999 New York Drama Critics Circle Award for Best Foreign Play. Four lives intertwine over the course of four and a half years in this densely plotted, stinging look at modern love and betrayal. "CLOSER is a sad, savvy, often funny play that casts a steely, unblinking gaze at the world of relationships and lets you come to your own conclusions ... CLOSER does not merely hold your attention; it burrows into you." *–New York Magazine* "A powerful, darkly funny play about the cosmic collision between the sun of love and the comet of desire." *–Newsweek Magazine* [2M, 2W] ISBN: 0-8222-1722-8

★ **THE MOST FABULOUS STORY EVER TOLD by Paul Rudnick.** A stage manager, headset and prompt book at hand, brings the house lights to half, then dark, and cues the creation of the world. Throughout the play, she's in control of everything. In other words, she's either God, or she thinks she is. "Line by line, Mr. Rudnick may be the funniest writer for the stage in the United States today ... One-liners, epigrams, withering put-downs and flashing repartee: These are the candles that Mr. Rudnick lights instead of cursing the darkness ... a testament to the virtues of laughing ... and in laughter, there is something like the memory of Eden." *–The NY Times* "Funny it is ... consistently, rapaciously, deliriously ... easily the funniest play in town." *–Variety* [4M, 5W] ISBN: 0-8222-1720-1

★ **A DOLL'S HOUSE by Henrik Ibsen, adapted by Frank McGuinness.** Winner of the 1997 Tony Award for Best Revival. "New, raw, gut-twisting and gripping. Easily the hottest drama this season." *–USA Today* "Bold, brilliant and alive." *–The Wall Street Journal* "A thunderclap of an evening that takes your breath away." *–Time Magazine* [4M, 4W, 2 boys] ISBN: 0-8222-1636-1

★ **THE HERBAL BED by Peter Whelan.** The play is based on actual events which occurred in Stratford-upon-Avon in the summer of 1613, when William Shakespeare's elder daughter was publicly accused of having a sexual liaison with a married neighbor and family friend. "In his probing new play, THE HERBAL BED ... Peter Whelan muses about a sidelong event in the life of Shakespeare's family and creates a finely textured tapestry of love and lies in the early 17th-century Stratford." *–The NY Times* "It is a first rate drama with interesting moral issues of truth and expediency." *–The NY Post* [5M, 3W] ISBN: 0-8222-1675-2

★ **SNAKEBIT by David Marshall Grant.** A study of modern friendship when put to the test. "... a rather smart and absorbing evening of water-cooler theater, the intimate sort of Off-Broadway experience that has you picking apart the recognizable characters long after the curtain calls." *– The NY Times* "Off-Broadway keeps on presenting us with compelling reasons for going to the theater. The latest is SNAKEBIT, David Marshall Grant's smart new comic drama about being thirtysomething and losing one's way in life." *–The NY Daily News* [3M, 1W] ISBN: 0-8222-1724-4

★ **A QUESTION OF MERCY by David Rabe.** The Obie Award-winning playwright probes the sensitive and controversial issue of doctor-assisted suicide in the age of AIDS in this poignant drama. "There are many devastating ironies in Mr. Rabe's beautifully considered, piercingly clear-eyed work ..." *–The NY Times* "With unsettling candor and disturbing insight, the play arouses pity and understanding of a troubling subject ... Rabe's provocative tale is an affirmation of dignity that rings clear and true." *–Variety* [6M, 1W] ISBN: 0-8222-1643-4

★ **DIMLY PERCEIVED THREATS TO THE SYSTEM by Jon Klein.** Reality and fantasy overlap with hilarious results as this unforgettable family attempts to survive the nineties. "Here's a play whose point about fractured families goes to the heart, mind – and ears." *–The Washington Post* "... an end-of-the-millennium comedy about a family on the verge of a nervous breakdown ... Trenchant and hilarious ..." *–The Baltimore Sun* [2M, 4W] ISBN: 0-8222-1677-9

DRAMATISTS PLAY SERVICE, INC.
440 Park Avenue South, New York, NY 10016 212-683-8960 Fax 212-213-1539
postmaster@dramatists.com www.dramatists.com

NEW PLAYS

★ HONOUR by Joanna Murray-Smith. In a series of intense confrontations, a wife, husband, lover and daughter negotiate the forces of passion, history, responsibility and honour. "HONOUR makes for surprisingly interesting viewing. Tight, crackling dialogue (usually played out in punchy verbal duels) captures characters unable to deal with emotions ... Murray-Smith effectively places her characters in situations that strip away pretense." *–Variety* "... the play's virtues are strong: a distinctive theatrical voice, passionate concerns ... HONOUR might just capture a few honors of its own." *–Time Out Magazine* [1M, 3W] ISBN: 0-8222-1683-3

★ MR. PETERS' CONNECTIONS by Arthur Miller. Mr. Miller describes the protagonist as existing in a dream-like state when the mind is "freed to roam from real memories to conjectures, from trivialities to tragic insights, from terror of death to glorying in one's being alive." With this memory play, the Tony Award and Pulitzer Prize-winner reaffirms his stature as the world's foremost dramatist. "... a cross between Joycean stream-of-consciousness and Strindberg's dream plays, sweetened with a dose of William Saroyan's philosophical whimsy ... CONNECTIONS is most intriguing ..." *–The NY Times* [5M, 3W] ISBN: 0-8222-1687-6

★ THE WAITING ROOM by Lisa Loomer. Three women from different centuries meet in a doctor's waiting room in this dark comedy about the timeless quest for beauty – and its cost. "... THE WAITING ROOM ... is a bold, risky melange of conflicting elements that is ... terrifically moving ... There's no resisting the fierce emotional pull of the play." *–The NY Times* "... one of the high points of this year's Off-Broadway season ... THE WAITING ROOM is well worth a visit." *–Back Stage* [7M, 4W, flexible casting] ISBN: 0-8222-1594-2

★ THE OLD SETTLER by John Henry Redwood. A sweet-natured comedy about two church-going sisters in 1943 Harlem and the handsome young man who rents a room in their apartment. "For all of its decent sentiments, THE OLD SETTLER avoids sentimentality. It has the authenticity and lack of pretense of an Early American sampler." *–The NY Times* "We've had some fine plays Off-Broadway this season, and this is one of the best." *–The NY Post* [1M, 3W] ISBN: 0-8-222-1642-6

★ THE LAST TRAIN TO NIBROC by Arlene Hutton. In 1940 two young strangers share a seat on a train bound east only to find their paths will cross again. "All aboard. LAST TRAIN TO NIBROC is a sweetly told little chamber romance." *–Show Business* "... [a] gently charming little play, reminiscent of Thorton Wilder in its look at rustic Americans who are to be treasured for their simplicity and directness ..." *–Associated Press* "The old formula of boy wins girls, boy loses girl, boy wins girl still works ... [a] well-made play that perfectly captures a slice of small-town-life-gone-by." *–Back Stage* [1M, 1W] ISBN: 0-8222-1753-8

★ OVER THE RIVER AND THROUGH THE WOODS by Joe DiPietro. Nick sees both sets of his grandparents every Sunday for dinner. This is routine until he has to tell them that he's been offered a dream job in Seattle. The news doesn't sit so well. "A hilarious family comedy that is even funnier than his long running musical revue *I Love You, You're Perfect, Now Change*." *–Back Stage* "Loaded with laughs every step of the way." *–Star-Ledger* [3M, 3W] ISBN: 0-8222-1712-0

★ SIDE MAN by Warren Leight. 1999 Tony Award winner. This is the story of a broken family and the decline of jazz as popular entertainment. "... a tender, deeply personal memory play about the turmoil in the family of a jazz musician as his career crumbles at the dawn of the age of rock-and-roll ..." *–The NY Times* "[SIDE MAN] is an elegy for two things – a lost world and a lost love. When the two notes sound together in harmony, it is moving and graceful ..." *–The NY Daily News* "An atmospheric memory play...with crisp dialogue and clearly drawn characters ... reflects the passing of an era with persuasive insight ... The joy and despair of the musicians is skillfully illustrated." *–Variety* [5M, 3W] ISBN: 0-8222-1721-X

DRAMATISTS PLAY SERVICE, INC.
440 Park Avenue South, New York, NY 10016 212-683-8960 Fax 212-213-1539
postmaster@dramatists.com www.dramatists.com